When a Perfect Woman Falls from Grace

When a Perfect Woman Falls from Grace

And How She Found the Light

Linda Sue McCall, LCSW

Linda Sue McCall
Lawrenceville, Georgia

The writings in this manuscript are as they are remembered by the author and not meant to belittle, judge, or harm anyone mentioned. Several chapters have specifics that might be upsetting and might trigger feelings and emotions that may be unresolved with some readers; please keep this in mind and seek the assistance needed.

This book is not intended to replace the need for therapy or counseling. Opinions in this book are provided for informational purposes only and are not intended as a substitute for the therapeutic acknowledgment or advice of a competent and knowledgeable counselor, social worker, or psychologist/psychiatrist. The reader should always consult a trusted licensed practitioner in matters relating to his/her health and particularly with respect to any condition that may require immediate medical/clinical attention. The information provided in this book should not be construed as personal medical or clinical advice or instruction. Self-diagnosis and self-treatment are not recommended and may indeed be detrimental. Readers who fail to consult competent, trusted, trained therapists or doctors assume the total risk of any injuries or illnesses resulting.

Definitions within the text are given from the perspective of the author and in layman's terms. Any specifics regarding various therapies and therapeutic processes are to be researched by the reader for more in-depth interpretations and understanding.

Copyright © 2015 by Linda Sue McCall

All rights reserved. No part of this book may be reproduced or transmitted in any form or by any means, electronic or mechanical, including photocopying, recording, or any information storage and retrieval system, without permission in writing from the author.

ISBN: 978-0-9962597-0-5

10 9 8 7 6 5 4 3 2   03 30 15

Printed in the United States of America

∞ This paper meets the requirements of ANSI/NISO Z39.48-1992 (Permanence of Paper)

This book is dedicated to Lyndsey.
Were it not for you, this book would never have been written.
And to Mom, who told me many times, "You can do anything."
You were right. Thank you for the powerful message.

Contents

Author's Note	ix
Opening Prayer	xi
Acknowledgments	xv
Introduction	xvii

Part I: Perfection

Chapter One:	Perfection	3
Chapter Two:	My Family	7
Chapter Three:	Gifts from My Family	15
Chapter Four:	My Perfection	21
Chapter Five:	Falling from Grace	29

Part II: Revisiting My Past

Chapter Six:	Embrace Therapy	35
Chapter Seven:	Become Educated	47
Chapter Eight:	Be Clear in Religion/Spirituality	53
Chapter Nine:	Make Peace with Losses	63
Chapter Ten:	Release the Toxicity	69

Chapter Eleven:	Be There for Another	79
Chapter Twelve:	Be Aware of Sensory Connections	85
Chapter Thirteen:	Learn from Synchronicity	97
Chapter Fourteen:	Assert Clear Boundaries	103
Chapter Fifteen:	Find Creativity	107
Chapter Sixteen:	Make Self-Care a Top Priority	111
Chapter Seventeen:	Become Grounded	115
Chapter Eighteen:	Take Action	119
Chapter Nineteen:	Find Laughter in Mistakes	125
Chapter Twenty:	See Clearly	129

Finding the Light   135
About the Author   137

Author's Note

When a Perfect Woman Falls from Grace is written in two distinct parts. The first provides background information on my family of origin, and the second part focuses on the process that I went through in order to find my way to the light. None of the fifteen chapters in part two is chronological, and they can be read separately, as they do not build on the previous ones.

My life has not been linear; through the years, the many doors I went through to find myself took me back to various time periods that were not sequential and, therefore, could not be written as such. Each of the fifteen chapters is about addressing specific issues that triggered me back to events in my childhood and as an adult that needed to be processed to move forward.

Opening Prayer

Dear God, Holy Spirit, and Beloved Angels,

I ask that you hear this prayer. May you surround your presence bright around all who read these words. May there be transformation to those seeking the light out of their dark places and spaces in time. May you grant them a new day to brighten their lives in a different way much more than they ever imagined. May you be with them, love them, guide them, and protect them on their journey while on this earth. And so it is.

Amen.

A dear, intuitive, gifted mentor and friend of mine said a similar prayer with me some three years ago when I was in a dark space and time. The prayer and her teachings helped me to find my way back to the light and have peace more quickly than if I had not spent the needed time with her. My belief is that it is ultimately up to each of us and God—as we know and see God, depending on our beliefs—to regain strength and bounce back to an equilibrium.

Finding the light is the key phrase that comes to my mind. Simply, either we develop the needed tools to get us through the hard times or we do not. All of us, if we live long enough, go through valleys and hard times. It is therefore our ability to gain perspective through the difficulties we have and adapt to live a life of light, which determines whether we have the ability to bounce back or to sink deep into a black abyss.

As a woman, mother, social worker, and therapist with many lived experiences, I find that it is only through my own healing that I have found for myself that I can truly help others and be present on a deep level. It is also through the sharing of my personal stories that I have been able to receive guidance from professionals and, therefore, become able to assist others to gain a deeper understanding of themselves. Through writing this book, it is my hope that many will be able to step away from the difficulties in their lives and choose to make positive decisions that will not only change their lives forever, but help them to start a new way of life.

As you read this book, you will see many examples of how my life has changed from who I was to who I have become. You will also see clearly how the changes that occurred in my life can and will impact others. The depth of the stories is from my reality and perspective, and the stories are all true. I am convinced that in sharing the knowledge of my challenges, it will serve not only to help those with whom I have personal connections, but also provide answers and a path for many men and women who struggle with the same issues. It will also give aid to many of the men, women, family members, and friends who want desperately to help and understand the ones they love. As you read these pages, you may surprisingly see some of the same characteristics in yourself or your loved ones.

Opening Prayer

It is my desire that sharing my knowledge that there are answers and help available will give you hope, confidence, and a better understanding of the challenges ahead and how change can ultimately occur and last.

Through my willingness to open up the very personal parts of my life, the hope is that others in need can begin to embrace healing, live in the present as opposed to the past, and be open to a brighter future. I believe the changes must start with us, individually and then collectively. We have been given the gift of life, and it is now time to band together to create peace and harmony among the lives on this planet. These writings are about opportunities for healing for many in a great and wonderful way.

If on your journey you have been seeking a book of total authenticity, you have now found it. Whether you choose to put it on the shelf or share it with someone you love is totally up to you. If you read further and embrace the lens through which I now view life, life for you can be not only a new beginning of light, but a life of joy and an abundance of miracles. Relax now; you have finally met your destination.

Acknowledgments

First and foremost, I want to thank my wonderful children, Aidan, Dustin, and Lyndsey, for their unwavering love and support, as well as their tolerance over the years. I love you more than you will ever know. Also, I want to thank my mother, who has blessed me beyond measure and who has been available to me as much as possible until the illness a few years ago claimed her mind. My gratitude goes to my closest family, especially my siblings and my niece Cheryl, and many others who are still present in body and mind, as well as those who are no longer present in the flesh but will always be in my heart. Thank you all for your love that has truly gotten me to where I am today.

Special thanks goes to Dr. Suzanne Carr, Rita Boestfleisch, Diane Zimberoff, David Hartman, and the many teachers, instructors, and colleagues of the Wellness Institute based in Issaquah, Washington, that had a significant impact on my life. Much gratitude goes to the instructors of the Eye Movement Desensitization and Reprocessing (EMDR) therapy training and to Dr. Francine Shapiro, who had the foresight to see the value in such a forward-thinking therapy. I want to thank two of my former supervisors, friends, and colleagues who have been, for the last twenty-five years, just a phone call away and have blessed my life more than they will ever know: Jewell Powell and Barbara Wilson. I want to give a special thanks to my former supervisor Ann Burdges, who blessed me by approving payment for and allowing time off for valuable training that changed my life forever. Also, I want to thank my dear friend and colleague Mary Blanford, who has been a loyal friend over the years. Many thanks goes to my many friends and colleagues who are currently in my life for giving me the gifts of love and support over the past three years that have allowed me to be transparent as I move forward in my calling.

Many thanks goes to the wonderful employees of BookLogix, especially Kelly Nightingale, Jessica Parker, Ellina Dent, and Daren Fowler for making this book have the professional presentation that it has today. But most of all, for helping me to make my dream of finishing this book a reality.

Introduction

Undoubtedly, you do not know me. You might have crossed my path as an acquaintance, relative, friend, colleague, coworker, teacher, client, or someone else, but you still do not know me. To add more confusion, I could tell you my name is Linda Sue McCall, but there are many Linda Sue McCalls in Georgia and even more in South Carolina where I grew up. You see, I have never told anyone who I am or what I am really about until now. So to begin, allow me to introduce myself. My name is Linda Sue McCall. My father named me some five decades ago in a small-town hospital in Seneca, South Carolina. My mother wanted so much to name me after her mother who had passed away when my mother was just a teenager. My mother was twenty-five years old when she gave birth to me. I was the youngest of six and her last child. My grandmother's name was Etta LaVienna (I think the spelling is correct but my Mom pronounced "Etta" as "Etter"). I thank my dad for intervening—if somehow he can hear me—because I do really like my name. My father tended to be a controlling man who left this earth some thirty years ago, but I still love him dearly and I always will. In fact, I love him more every time I think of what my name could have been (just teasing). Linda

Sue is a fine name. Not that Etta LaVienna is a bad name at all. I think I just like the very common name of Linda Sue. Sadly though, I remember while writing this that I was my mother's last hope of having a child named after someone she loved very, very dearly and deeply. Being the youngest and remembering how she told me of wanting a namesake for her mother through her daughters, I am certain she wanted to name my other sisters after her mom as well. With her being the southern, passive woman that she was, she succumbed to my father's desire to name me.

My five siblings and I grew up on the Mountain, as we sometimes called it, in a rural community called Mountain Rest. It was really at the foothills of the Blue Ridge Mountains and very country. Many times over the years, I have told friends and acquaintances that I thought the word "ruined" was "ruint" until I finished high school; they see it as a joke, and it is funny in some ways, but it really is true. On the Mountain, there were square dances every Saturday night at the local state park and country music played on the weekends at the local grocery store. I grew up hearing banjos and fiddles, and I knew how to square dance.

It is beautiful there, and in my family, my brother Dan referenced that small pocket of land in South Carolina as "God's Country," and my family still calls it that to this very day. When the wind blows, it is as if the trees speak of peace and harmony, and the beauty of the sunrise and sunset through the trees is breathtaking. The stars at night fill the skies with their luminescent, spectacular constellations, and the air is so clean and pure that one can really feel the air in their bodies like the first deep breath taken in the morning on the top of a mountain in the wintertime with sparkles of pureness all around. The crickets chirp at night, playing their own music and repetitive mantras as the fireflies light up the sky in the summertime. It is home and a place to be the envy of many.

Introduction

But for me, I do not plan to live there again; the first twenty years of my life were spent there. It is not that I do not love nature, because I surely do. I love farms and farm animals—really, I love animals of any kind. It is not that I do not love my family nor that I do not miss them. I love them and miss them all very much. It is just that the Atlanta area in Georgia has become my home. The two-hour drive to visit my family in Mountain Rest is perfect for me to be able to come back home and sleep in my own bed after I visit for the day. It is a boundary of distance that serves me most in my healing, as I am no longer controlled by the sad memories of the past. When I go back to God's Country, I am triggered by how things were for me as a child, and when I come back to Georgia, breathe the air at my home in the suburban area of Atlanta, and see the city lights, I feel blessed. I am blessed and I am grateful.

There is much to tell about my life, as there is for everyone. We all have our own unique stories. To be perfectly honest, I never planned to tell my story or share the stories in the writing of this book or any book. My life has been very private and few, and I do mean very few, know the parts of my life I am now sharing. The intense desire to share my path and spread the word with you has been given to me as a divine calling, much like ministers who are called by God to preach, and it is unexplainable. The word that comes to my mind as I write this is "healing," and the healing that has occurred in my own life and in the lives of others as I have been able to help. In this book, I am offering a vision on how individuals who feel that they have to be perfect, can get to where they want to go emotionally for their own happiness and peace, by releasing the bondage of the past. Without directions, a map, or a guide from someone who has journeyed the path, anyone can get lost and stray from the destination and never find the way. For many, I have become a bridge in their healing. In my own healing, I have been fortunate to have been led, taught, supervised, and mentored by some of the best bridges in the world and, for that, I am thankful.

You are invited into my life for the details of my experiences. By knowing parts of my story and some examples of how I have helped others, you will find that you and/or your loved ones can do the same. But beware, before you venture further it may just change your life forever.

As they say in God's Country:
May God Bless You,
Linda Sue McCall
(Thanks to my dad)

Part I
Perfection

Chapter One

Perfection

In my counseling career helping women and men consumed with perfectionism, I have found that the behaviors do not need to be defined; they know what they are and sometimes they even know the cost of these behaviors. In seeking my own understanding around the definition of perfection, the one of being flawless rings true and is most descriptive. Someone who strives for perfection all the time is someone who buys into the idea that he or she must adopt a behavior that is above and beyond what is typically expected and certainly beyond having balance in one's life. Many faiths, religions, and other spiritual practices believe in saints, gods, and goddesses. In the Christian faith, the one with which I am most familiar, the only person who ever lived and was perfect on earth was Jesus Christ. Therefore, if no human being other than Christ has been perfect, the question remains as to why so many of us are consumed with being perfect. The bottom line, as I have come to know and understand, is that it is an underlying, unrealistic belief that one can never achieve. It is a goal not to be fully obtained.

For some clients I have provided therapy for, the concept of perfection is giving up one's self for the expectations of others and, in so doing, giving up what they hold as true and authentic about themselves. For many, it means to be something and someone they are not in order to please others. For others, it is about "being good" in every way, which results in only receiving love based on performance. This can be by not disappointing someone or even calling attention to a perceived flaw or need because typically there is a basic unspoken, or at times spoken, understanding that when performance falls short, there is sure to be abandonment, neglect, trauma, abuse, or another high cost. For yet others, perfection is about never having enough or never being secure enough with basic needs and feeling the stress and responsibility to go above and beyond what would be considered by others to be a balanced, normal way of life.

Perfection is a part of all socio-economic levels and all cultures. There are none that are exempt from this role, and, in many cultures, it is more ingrained than in others. The cost is great and it affects many of the world who are leaders, solid and steadfast. They are often the successful, the driven, and always, the "go to" individuals. Many pay a tremendous price in not developing a true sense of self, and in so doing, they have given their power to others to define them and to live their lives from that perspective. This is sometimes noticed through various addictions, and one that is especially prevalent for perfectionism is workaholism. But, regardless of what it is, they lack balance in their lives. Balance means a time for work but not constantly working and finding time for themselves, their family and friends, and time for relaxation and to have fun. It is not uncommon for those with perfection tendencies to work many more hours than most and certainly more than their salaries cover.

Working with individual clients coming to me for counseling over the years, I have found that perfectionist ways are more common in those who have experienced traumatic events, but not always. The overarching consensus is that the individual either experienced abuse in some way or fashion and/or they did not have their needs met at a young age. From my professional experience, I have found perfection to be emotional and sensory by usually having a negative effect on one's ability to feel joy and contentment and impacting one's ability to physically feel whole and healthy. Many of the emotions and feelings described to me in sessions are fear based and/or shame and guilt based with too much time going by without the issues being addressed, and usually whatever occurred to encourage perfectionism begins in early stages of development. Remembering some of my client's stories, some experienced sexual abuse, domestic violence, other types of abuse and neglect, natural disasters, and other events that unraveled their sense of being safe; others simply may have been so isolated that no one was available to them to validate their feelings as being real. The fear and/or shame and guilt remained, thus it became generalized to not being safe within their environments and not being safe within themselves. Perfection became the focus with secrets, a common and instrumental part of staying safe, which started and/or continued a cycle of dysfunction. With no way out of the façade, some describe it as if the earth became unbalanced and unstable; it was as if there were an earthquake lying dormant underneath with no knowledge of when it was going to occur or how high the earthquake would be on the Richter scale.

When one becomes more present and aware that this is being experienced, it will require safety and a rebuilding of one's life; the best way to view this would be in finding good architects to assist in constructing a new structure to withstand the traumas, storms, and earthquakes of life. The best way to further explain this is to make the goal of authenticity number one with the desire to start a new life through the willingness to be vulnerable, open, and honest, not only to gain knowledge of what one's needs are, but how to get one's needs met.

Chapter Two
My Family

In my family of origin, there were many good times and bad times. Much of what I am sharing with you in these writings are the difficulties so that you can get a clearer picture of how I might have chosen a life of perfection. From observation of my family dynamics and my own experiences, many of the situations described could have led to a life of choosing perfection. Let's just say I had many opportunities to develop an unhealthy way of life. One interesting rule of my family was that we were never to speak in a positive manner about ourselves. If we had an achievement, it was to be kept silent. There was no room for boasting or bragging or having a "big head." Thinking highly of ourselves was considered conceited and that we thought we were better than others, which was unacceptable. We were to be humble at all times and to "be proud of what and where we came from" regardless of how embarrassing it may have been—it was *our* way of life.

In my immediate family, there were six children, four girls and two boys, with me being the youngest. My father and mother came from families in which each was one of nine children. My father was the second oldest in a family of eight boys and one girl, and my mother was the youngest of five girls and four boys.

From what my mother told me as a child, when my father was born he weighed approximately two pounds and was not expected to live. He was a miracle that my grandmother took care of and nursed into continued life when most children at that birth weight in the 1920s didn't make it. My mother on the other hand was born at home and never even had a birth certificate or record of birth until adulthood. We have no idea how much she weighed or anything about her birth. Both my mother and father's families were considered hardworking but very poverty-stricken. My mother had four brothers, one was not usually employed and one had difficulty keeping a job. These two brothers were the ones that my mother cooked and cared for at home, once the other children in her family left. My mother had sayings and rhymes she would quote to help us understand the way life was and one example of such is, "A man works from sun to sun, but a woman's work is never done." This was her way of teaching us how life was supposed to be or perhaps how she developed her own self-limiting beliefs or maybe even how she justified how things were.

The story of how my parents got married was that my father was kicked out of his home (I am not sure why) and came to live at my mother's home. My grandmother on my mother's side was known to be very giving, loving, and nurturing, and she took this homeless man into her home. I am not sure how long afterwards but my father asked my grandmother for my mother's hand in marriage, and she signed for my mother to get married. My mother told of being very young, either fourteen or fifteen, while my father was nineteen. From the stories my mother told, my grandmother wanted my mother to have "a life away from being a slave to her brothers." Even though I am unclear as to what all the rationale was about, I surmised that her brothers were abusive to my mother and my grandmother wanted her to have the opportunity to get away from it and have a life with a man that my grandmother respected.

My Family

There was no question; my grandmother did respect my father. He was known for his goodness and for being honest and hardworking. On some level, I believe my grandmother knew she had a serious illness and would not be alive much longer, and she probably needed to know that my mother would be financially cared for upon her death. My grandmother died a little over a year afterwards but, to this day, no one knows what took her life. Being so poor and without healthcare, there was little done to prevent early deaths back then. My mother was emotionally so close to my grandmother that I do not think she ever fully recovered from her death. Every time she spoke of her, sadness would come over her, and whether she voiced it or not, we all knew how much she missed our grandmother.

The only living grandparent I knew was my grandmother on my father's side. All of my other grandparents had passed on before my birth. Grandmother McCall was stern and tough and was not really close to anyone except her youngest son, Joe, who she voiced that she loved dearly. She did sew a dress for me once when I was very young and had not done so for my siblings, so I was thought of as her favorite. I am not really sure that is accurate. I think she, like many others, did not show or was not even aware of her true feelings. Somehow I feel she was caught up in her own perfectionism. But I am honored that she cared about me through the gift of that dress, and with that act of kindness, she let me know.

My brothers, sisters, and I were raised in a very small house, like a typical ranch-style home, about 1200 square feet with only one bathroom and a front and back porch. The house was in the middle of approximately six acres, where we had cows, pigs, chickens, cats and dogs, and wild animals from time to time. We had a huge garden on one side of the house and the back. We had a very large clothesline at the opposite side of the house from the garden, and a large barn in the back of the house. Our home was ours, and there was no debt associated with it; my mother often told us that our father worked night and day to pay off our house in two years. She would say, "We might not have much, but we do have a home."

My sister Jean was the oldest. She was more like a mother to me than a sister and took care of me as long as I can remember as a child. One of my first memories was of her carrying me on her hip as our father and uncles were adding a room onto our small home. With this addition, the girls would finally have their own bedroom, and that was wonderful! Jean talked of having our own space and that being like a dream come true. Jean was good and was beautiful, especially to me. She did all the right things by our standards; she went to church and studied her Bible daily. She taught Sunday school and was loved by the family and the community. She watched her weight and exercised often. She did many of the chores at home and never complained. Often she stayed up very late at night studying; it was not unusual for her to be up at two in the morning studying. And she would get up at five or five thirty to help mother with breakfast and get us ready for school. My mother used to tell the story of Jean crying as a baby and being allergic to her breast milk. In fact, my parents were told by the local doctor to raise her on condensed milk, and that was her food for the first few months of her life. Now I cringe to think about how malnourished she must have been. Anyway, Jean finished high school, married afterwards, and moved to Florida. It was sad for her to leave, but I felt that her life would be better away from home. Little did I know what was to come.

My brother Dan was next in line and a year younger than Jean. He was something else, to say the least! Some might refer to him as a character, and that he was. If there was trouble, he found it or it found him. I am not exactly sure if he created it or attracted it, but he was known for being full of energy and mischief. He had a full head of red hair and the rest of us had dark hair, so he was always noticed. I think he liked his hair color as an adult, but I am not so sure as a child. Dan had one major goal in life and that was to be like our dad.

My Family

In fact, many of the behaviors our dad had, he did not want Dan to replicate, but Dan did anyway.

Dan worked hard, but he loved to hunt and fish, with or without our dad, and was excellent at shooting and bringing home game to eat. There was not much Dan couldn't do. When Dan was in high school, he began smoking like our dad. I remember waking up in the middle of the night with him crying, screaming, and begging Mom to give back his cigarettes. We were all told to go back to bed, and then the cigarettes were never discussed again, but were allowed. Sometime around the year Dan finished high school, he got up early one morning and drove the tractor to another man's house at dad's request. We received a call that Dan was in an accident, and the tractor had turned over. My dad brought him home about an hour later with blood all over him and a horrible cut on the side of his head where we could see his skull. My mother kept yelling at dad to take him to the doctor's office, but dad had to make sure Dan changed his clothes and washed the blood off before leaving the house. Looking back, I am sure my father's own perfectionism got in the way of his judgment. I remember being afraid I would never see Dan again, but he did return home and fully recovered. Within the year after Dan graduated from high school, he was drafted into the Army and the family was devastated. Then we found out that he only had one kidney, and we were totally confused that the Army took him without a kidney. This was not supposed to happen…but it did. Fortunately, Dan was sent to Germany not Vietnam, where most of his friends were, and we were relieved. Germany was not so great for him either, and he was glad to return home after fulfilling his two-year draft commitment.

Gail was the next in line and five years older than me. She was beautiful like Jean, and for whatever reason, Gail had my father's attention no matter what. They had a wonderful saying together, "friends to the end," and we all felt that she was his favorite. My mother told me that after Gail's birth, she went into a deep depression and had to be hospitalized; I surmise it was probably postpartum depression. During this time, Gail was cared for by an aunt and uncle while mom stabilized. Afterwards, when my mom was discharged from the hospital, this aunt and uncle did not want to give Gail back and asked my Dad to give Gail to them. Of course, my father refused, but I often wondered if he had an underlying fear that he would lose Gail somehow. Interestingly, I see many of Dad's qualities in Gail; she always seemed to have Dad's positive qualities—she manages money very well, certainly better than most of us, and was tough when she needed to be and soft when the situation required it. She is probably one of the best female carpenters ever. And she had less trouble saying "no" to others than the rest of us. We did see that our father was typically hard on Gail when she did something outside of what he had given her permission to do; it may have been because she did so little without his permission. Once, when Gail was in high school taking Cosmetology, she came home with her hair frosted (gray and black), and I thought the world was going to end for all of us, but especially for her. Our father was furious! Needless to say, the next day her hair was fully dark again. Dad stated repeatedly that Gail had promised not to do anything permanent and one of our uncles (they were always stirring up stuff and we were often mad at them for the things they told dad because it was usually at a cost to us) told him that it was permanent hair color, so his position was that Gail had disobeyed him. At that time, I decided it was more than okay not to be his favorite, but it was never okay to disobey him. I was traumatized by the way he acted. Like so many issues in our family, we never spoke of it. That night was one of many times that had come before and would come again.

Next were my twin brother and sister, Royce and Joyce. In childhood, they were inseparable, and being two years older than me, there was no way I won any argument or minor disagreement. My sister Joyce had a hernia at birth and a few weeks later had surgery. My mother relived this occurrence many times with us and was especially close to and overprotective of Joyce. She expressed a lot of fear that she almost lost Joyce as a baby. Joyce was pretty, thin, and popular. I must admit, I was a little jealous of her. I always believed that she got away with more than me. I always got caught when we did something wrong whether she did or not. With her around, I was always second best. She seemed to always get the best grades and the most attention from the nicest looking boys, and just seemed to have it all. One night after Joyce had finished high school, she had come home late, and I woke up to hearing her screaming and crying in the front yard. Dan and Joyce had gone out on a double date, and my father had been drinking, of course. From what I could tell, Dad had slapped Joyce and told her to leave. Dan had Joyce get back into his car, and neither of them ever came back home to live again. They rented a small house a few miles from ours. I was sad to see them go and never understood what happened to Joyce that night, and she never told. When I asked, she would say, "You know how dad is and I love him anyways."

Her twin, Royce, was handsome, warm, and always sensitive. He was very different from the other males in our family. He was not interested in fishing, hunting, or farming, but he did what he had to do as a male in the family. Royce instead liked to read and loved to learn. He was more fixed on doing well in school and dreaming about how things could be different than enjoying and settling on how they were. He seemed to want more than to make the best of a bad situation. At one time, I thought he would be a Baptist preacher, and he did preach a few sermons, but he chose a different path. Royce and I were the last two at home for a few years, so we became rather close during that time. Even though I missed our other siblings, it was nice to bond with him. When Royce married and left, he would be away for months without visiting us at home. My mother would tell me as she and I cried, longing for Royce, "A son is a son until he takes a wife, but a daughter is a daughter all of her life." To me, as I internalized this saying, this was her way of saying that we couldn't do anything about it, but I, as a daughter, was never to do the same.

Then there was me, the youngest of six. At birth, I was close to ten pounds, and it was a difficult birth for my mother, especially since at that time in history few births were caesarean. From most books written about children growing up in alcoholic homes, I could have been considered the "lost child"—the one that no one paid attention to. Yet, even though that may have been somewhat of my role as a child, I was too unusual to be the one who stayed lost. Interestingly, none of my life has been accidental, even though I have thought that many times; I now know how divinely guided it has been. In writing this book and being open and vulnerable to all, I can fulfill my calling at the deepest level and that is certainly not by accident.

Chapter Three
Gifts from My Family

A couple of years ago, I wrote most of this chapter with information I was willing to share with others at the time. It was the beginning of me coming to terms with sharing with others my past of perfection enough to write it down and talk about a small part of it. I didn't expect for it to have the impact on others that it did. When I realized the significance, I knew that God was leading me on a path to share more. The assignment to share of myself in a small way was difficult two and a half years ago. Now the courage to share this chapter of my life is easy in comparison to the other chapters. The gifts shared here are an introduction to the positives that often come from the negative or hard times in our lives. My mother always said, "Every cloud has a silver lining" and I do believe that is true. This chapter is a glimpse of the challenges as well as the silver lining in growing up as I did.

Gifts received:

My life has been complex. In fact, so much has happened in my life, and so many things are so big that to even conceive that I could narrow down what I want to convey to anyone is a challenge. The last count of members in my family before I stopped counting was forty-two—which included my children, my parents, my siblings, and their families.

Growing up in a family of eight, I developed a strong sense of how to survive. My family was poor, and it took everything my parents made financially to feed and clothe the six children. Being the youngest, I received a lot of hand-me-downs. My mother was an excellent seamstress and worked in a sewing factory; she would make our clothes. I looked forward to Easter every year because that was the one time of the year when I had a new outfit; my mother would stay up all night the night before making our clothes so that we would have something new. My father was a carpenter, laborer, and a farmer and worked very hard; his hands were calloused and rough, and he was physically tired all the time.

My family's first gift to me:
1) No matter how hard times are, one carries on and moves forward.

Living in a three-bedroom home with one bathroom was difficult with three sisters and two brothers. We didn't complain to our parents much though. When my dad bought the house after my parents were first married, there was no indoor bathroom. Another challenge was we only had two mirrors in the house. With four girls, we would all vie for who got the mirror with the sink underneath; also, we needed a mirror with good lighting to put on our makeup and the only one in the house was in the bathroom, of course. I guess the one disagreement my siblings and I had the most was who got the bathroom next and for how long.

Another gift:
2) We realized early on that we're not the only people in the world and it is certainly not all about us. There are others that have needs as well.

I remember when we were called to the table for meals, and how even though my mom made sure we each had enough to eat, the ones who got to the table first got the biggest pieces of chicken. It was usually the chicken breast that went first, and not liking dark meat, you can bet after I figured this out, I got to the table first.

Another gift:
    3) If you want the best, you have to get to it first.

My mother had many dreams that she was unable to actualize due to being poor and having so many children at such a young age and her own self-limiting beliefs; yet she instilled many dreams and values in her children. There are statements she said, and I remember them clearly when challenges come my way. The one that had the most profound effect on me was, "you can do anything."

Next gift:
    4) You can do anything.

My mother and father made many tough decisions. Sometimes they made decisions based on fear and their own unmet needs. Even though we didn't understand them, we knew that they were doing the best they could.

Another gift:
    5) Life is not easy, and you have to make the tough decisions and do the best you can.

My father instilled in all of his children the importance of graduating from high school. There was no question his children would since only one of his eight siblings graduated from high school. My siblings and I did graduate from high school, all of us. Three went on to graduate with bachelor's degrees from college and one from graduate school, which was me.

Next gift:
    6) Graduating from school is important.

We truly lived off the land. We grew our own vegetables, had our own farm animals, and in fact, my brothers milked our own cows. My father was a very innovative man and would work for individuals in the community in exchange to use their land for large crops of field corn. The field corn was for the farm animals that he had planned to slaughter the next year for the meat to feed all of us. One summer, we had no rain and the crops were dying. I remember talking to my father, who was a man of very few words. I could tell he was worried. He talked of the lack of rain and of the need to get the crops to grow and then he said, "You know, this happens sometimes and then sometimes it rains." Not long afterwards, the rain came.

Another gift:
    7) Blessings come when we least expect them—you must have faith.

Oddly enough, neither of my parents went to church, but they were religious in their own ways. I think I knew many of the basic stories of the Bible before I ever started elementary school. They found opportunities to quote scripture frequently. One way in which they exercised their faith was to serve the community and to be available to others when there was an illness, death, accident, or need. My mother would always bake cakes or take food to those who were in need and/or suffering in some way, and my father would always be either pulling someone's car or farm animal out of a ditch or literally putting out a fire somewhere. In fact, many of the stories told at my father's funeral in 1984 were of wonderful things he had done and events that my siblings and I never even knew had taken place. Both of my parents were very humble.

Greatest gift:

    8) Serving others is life's greatest gift of all.

There are many other gifts I received from my family; many of which will be shared with you in chapters ahead. The contradictory side of the gifts were the lessons my siblings and I learned from the pain and the suffering in our family; this pain and suffering led to my life in the role of a perfect woman. There are many secrets that usually go unspoken and unwritten in families that keep them sick and dysfunctional, and ours was no different. It is the secrets and the shame and guilt around those secrets that continue patterns and cycles of addictions, trauma, pain, and dysfunction. For many who embrace the truth and are willing to have the courage to share, healing can begin. When secrets are brought out into the open, shame loses its power and individuals gain strength. But much, much more, when strength comes, doors open and light appears into a new beginning and a new life.

Chapter Four
My Perfection

I feel that I have lived many lifetimes in this one; if there is a positive side to this, it would be that I have compassion and understanding for those going through hardships and experiencing pain. My experiences put me in a position to understand on a deep level many different challenges others are going through. At the University of Georgia, in the school of social work, I was taught to have empathy; empathy was defined to me as being able to help someone going through an experience by having an understanding of where they had been even though I might not have similar experiences. Being able to put myself in someone else's shoes is not an area in which I am lacking. The fact is, from my own experiences, I am able to relate to many.

Some of my earlier years are times I try to forget. Some of my not wanting to remember may be due to memories of a horrible car accident my mother was in when I was very young; I still vividly remember her face all bruised and her body all bandaged. Many times, it has been said that children do not remember things when they are very young, but sometimes they do remember. For me, memories of many of the other traumatic events in my life are ones that I want to forget, and I am able to just force the memories from my mind. My elementary and middle school years were such times that I chose not to think about or remember. I guess in some way I believed that if I moved away from "God's Country" and lost contact with my childhood friends and extended family, my past would disappear—it never did.

It wasn't until the year 2000 that I became licensed as a clinical social worker, but the truth is... I had really been a social worker all of my life. To care for those who cannot or do not know how to take care of themselves and to advocate for social justice and fairness has always been at the forefront of my thinking and being as far back as I can remember.

From the beginning, I always knew that I was different from the others in my family and certainly different from many others' families. It wasn't always from a perspective of shame and feeling bad or defective, certainly that was a part of it, but it was from just having an inner knowing that I was different and maybe even what one might consider special in a good way. At times, being different was okay and positive, and other times it was not. Certainly, on the negative side, the arguments and conflicts in the home in which I grew up never made sense to me. Sometimes, I would even start the conflicts and the chaos, and that never made sense to me either. Early on, I did not know to question it; it was a way of life, and being powerless to change anything was the central theme of the family. I found myself always longing to be away from home but not knowing what that meant or how that might look. I wondered if I would ever be able to pull it off. On a subconscious level, I believe I really wanted to get away from myself, but I didn't even know who that person was to get away from, and more importantly, I did not know that I did not know. The old saying I heard many times, "Ignorance is bliss," certainly did not feel true with my life and me. I was miserable down deep inside, but no one knew, and I never felt the freedom to say it. I believed that if I did verbalize it, no one would listen. It was a façade, and I knew better than anyone how to mask my feelings. It was easy because my feelings were pushed so far away that I had no idea what I was feeling, and what's more, I had little desire to know.

In my family system, I liked being alone more than being with anyone else. Yet, I found it impossible to be alone most of the time. I shared a bedroom with three sisters, and during the day people were just everywhere. Looking back, I think our house was about 1,200 square feet after the room addition when I was a toddler. For eight people, that is not a lot of physical space. Additionally, my mother and father would take in our cousins and their parents when they needed a place to stay. Others visited us all the time. Our relatives would come in often and head for the kitchen to get a piece of bread or cake. My mother was excellent in the kitchen and put a lot of her love into her food. Since she had a reputation for her cooking skills and our house was open to any and all who wanted to eat and/or visit, it didn't seem to matter to anyone that came to our house that we had nothing of value except food. My parents were proud people and never let anyone know that we were in need of anything. We all grew up knowing we were to follow their example and do the same; it was a way of life.

In my loneliness, I developed a deep love of nature, the outdoors, and especially animals. There were lots of open spaces, and most of my waking hours were spent outside once I finished my chores. I was able to watch very few television programs, but we had three channels on that old Zenith Television. When we turned the outside pole with the antenna attached just right, we had good reception. The program I enjoyed the most was *I Love Lucy*. I had this wonderful little dog named Lucy Cricket who was my very best friend; when my father gave her to me as a young child, I named her after Lucille Ball and the crickets I loved to hear chirping at night. She was maybe twenty pounds and a bulldog/Chihuahua mix. The love in her eyes was unmatched to anything else; it was unconditional and consistent.

Her eyes were brown to everyone else, but to me, they were golden with sparkles of crystal fairy dust; and, when she looked at me, the sparkles would come my way, making my heart sing. She was with me from the time I was five years old until I was twelve. One day she never came home; that day was one of the saddest, most painful days of my life. Lucy Cricket was like an angel from God. We did everything together. She was my buddy, confidant, and best friend. We ate together, when my parents weren't watching of course. What I ate, she ate. She and I would hide under the bed, and we would share fatback biscuits at breakfast. I would take a bite and then she would. When I ate black walnuts, she would eat them too. She rescued me from the deep sadness and confusion I felt inside. She understood. No words ever had to be exchanged.

As time went on, significant changes happened, and I was always unprepared for them; I grew older, never knowing what would happen next, but knowing somehow that it would continue to worsen. I further developed fear and what some call a sense of hypervigilance and analyzing. I was always aware of my surroundings and made sure I was not in danger. Also, with my family being so over-extended, I did not want to add any hardships to what they were experiencing. It was as if I walked on eggshells, not knowing when the crack would be too loud or noticeable as I walked.

My fears and awareness of my surroundings continued to heighten as time went on. My oldest sister married and moved to Florida sometime in my elementary school years; she returned home about one and a half years later after being hospitalized for a devastating mental illness. She was a different person than when she left: her behaviors were out of control, and she was in and out of psychiatric hospitals due to her suicidal thoughts and attempts. My Lucy Cricket died. My father's drinking continued to spiral out of control. I had yet another traumatic experience by almost drowning in the lake at a local state park. There was "lack" of what my siblings and I needed everywhere; there was not enough time, not enough money, not enough security, love, or anything else. I went from one traumatic experience to another. My parents were suffering too. Sometime within the midst of the insanity of home life and the overwhelming losses, my schoolwork suffered—which looking back was inevitable— and I failed the fourth grade, which was a huge embarrassment to me. Not only did I feel that I did not fit in at home, I did not feel like I fit in anywhere in society. There were times I wish I could have hidden and just disappeared, but that wasn't even possible. With me always being very tall and overweight, by my mere size, there was no way to hide and nowhere to go. The thoughts and feelings of being exposed and vulnerable at all times were very present and were very negative. The secrets continued and expanded with me not wanting anyone to know me or anything about me. I didn't want anyone to know what was happening in my family and how much pain we were experiencing. The shame that comes from secrets and how I internalized things continued to be pervasive.

From the day I received the report card in the mail with the news of needing to repeat the fourth grade, I had a burning desire to prove myself and to pull myself out of the humiliation I had succumbed to. Being somewhat of an action person, having a diversion helped me to have a different focus from the insanity of home. It was important for me to show everyone that I was intelligent, even though I didn't believe it. At that time, what others thought of me was very important. Perhaps, the need to prove myself stemmed from shame around failing that grade, or it could have been due to my desire to win my father's approval or perhaps for some other reason, but I let everyone know that my goal and intention was to make up that grade I did not pass and to graduate with "my class."

In the years that followed, I continued to gain weight and was close to fifty pounds overweight the year before I was going to start middle school. My self-esteem was at an all-time low. So, the summer prior to seventh grade, I lost fifty pounds plus some. I was very thin and began to find out how the rest of the world existed—the thin part of the world. After starting to eat again, I would starve myself at times to keep my weight down, but then I would over-eat because I couldn't tolerate the constant gnawing feeling of the emptiness with the lack of food. The yo-yo syndrome way of eating and dieting became commonplace for me. I was gaining popularity due to being thin and being noticed, but no matter how many accolades I received for being thin and attractive, I felt emptiness inside. I would be at home or in social events at church or at family gatherings and still feel lonely.

In high school, I took a full load for three years and went to summer school. I was able to graduate with my class. The irony was that the class I graduated with was not really "my class." Focusing so hard on overcoming my failures and perceived failures, I failed to see the wonderful connections I had with my new friends, the students who were a year younger than me; they were "my class." Interesting how when we do certain things, the here and now is so often overlooked due to focus on the future. How different life would be if we lived in the present and valued each and every moment with gratitude. How different my life would have been . . .

My senior year in high school I fell in love. Following suit with what most women do in Mountain Rest, I always thought I would finish high school and get married. Since that relationship did not work out, I participated in a city beauty pageant, and surprisingly to my family and I, I won. My life became quite different afterwards. Prior to this pageant, I had decided that college was not something I was able to pursue; I never even thought of it as a possibility and certainly never thought I was smart enough to go to college. The scholarship money I won, however, had to go towards education, and since I had to compete in the state pageant a year later, I had to find a way to go to college, or a technical school at the very least. Since Criminal Justice was intriguing and I was really not interested in any other curriculum, I decided to go to a technical college and take classes. My brother Royce and my mom were two of my biggest fans. They told me I could succeed in school even though I didn't believe it; I carried on. That first year in college was difficult. I traveled on several weekends participating in pageants across the state and worked at jobs as much as possible. There was just not enough time, money, or energy to do all that others expected from me to be successful. I succumbed to the belief that my life had a life of its own and that the decisions were made and there was nothing I could do about it. The feeling of drifting, like being on a raft out in the ocean with no real destination, was ever present with me; everything had a domino effect, one thing would lead to another and the feeling of powerlessness was pervasive. It was like the occurrences in my life were somewhat accidental. I did not win or place in the state pageant. Afterwards, my father told me that I was a "sucker" to have even participated. The visceral feeling I had at that time was like I had been stabbed in the heart, yet another experience confirming that I was not perfect enough.

One year later, I graduated from the technical college I attended and received financial aid to go to a four year private college. Three years afterwards, I graduated with a bachelor's degree in psychology with a minor in criminal justice. Being a double major throughout the three years, I decided not to take the last class for a major in criminal justice, which was only offered once every two years. I decided to receive my degree in psychology and move on. While receiving my degree, I had gotten braces and jaw surgery to correct an overbite and had every intention of getting back into pageants to "prove myself"—which was always one of my mantras; I decided I would have a long-standing career in either singing or modeling or both. Afterwards, several events happened, and my dreams of success and a career of my choice became dreams of my past.

In my journey, I continued searching for answers. Prior to my healing, I held a great deal of anger inside, blamed and judged others, and had a hard time with forgiveness and letting go. Believing erroneously that I had control and needed to be in control, darkness engulfed me for much of my earlier years; I believe I made decisions subconsciously that it was normal to feel guilt, shame, sadness, fear, and anger on a regular basis. Furthermore, it became even more normal to me not feel anything at all.

Chapter Five
Falling from Grace

My mother used to tell my siblings and me the story from the Bible of an angel. Mostly, when I think of angels, I think of pure, good, perfect beings. Well, in the story, this angel had fallen from God's grace. This angel, to be known as Lucifer, was a beautiful angel from heaven and was the angel closest to God. This angel had everything: he was smart, beautiful, powerful, and perfect. But Lucifer had a problem, he wasn't satisfied and he wanted more; he wanted to be worshiped like God and even be above God. Once God figured this out, Lucifer was cast out of heaven and never allowed to return. Lucifer was stripped of his beauty, his standing with God, and of his place in heaven. Lucifer then became known as Satan. Lucifer, who was once known as the "son of the morning," being no longer humble, had fallen from grace.

As a child, being mesmerized by my mother's storytelling, I would question why and how this could ever happen to an angel in such a high place. I would think to myself that if I were ever to be in God's favor like this angel was I would never do anything to displease God. Afterwards, my mom would talk about how this never happens with us since Jesus came and died on the cross for our sins. She would say that God always forgives and that his "grace is sufficient." Honestly, there were times I believed that his grace was sufficient and times I did not.

There have been many times in my past when I haven't felt the presence of God; there have been many times when I believed that God had forsaken me or worse, but there has been only once that I remember when I truly felt I had fallen from his grace and was unlovable, even by God. So many things happened that were way beyond my scope of understanding. In the middle of suffering and having so little control as a child, I took on perfection and decided (without being aware) that if I am just good enough perhaps my life and the lives of others will be different. Little did I know that this very statement was a false and self-limiting belief.

As an adult, it finally clicked with me that changes needed to occur and that I was unable to continue in the same way anymore. I knew I either had to make changes or give up. It was black and white, all or nothing. Since giving up was never an option in my Christian upbringing, it was clear to me that it was up to me and that changes were in order. Oddly enough, no one even knew that I was at the bottom. Unlike individuals who are addicted to drugs or alcohol or who are in trouble with the law, it wasn't outwardly noticeable to others. It was apparent to me, though, that I had surely fallen from grace and was not lovable even to God; there was nothing that anyone could do. At first, I just wanted someone—anyone—to rescue me. I just could not continue in the same murky mess and feel the same way, and there was no one to blame.

When I finally hit the bottom I was dealing with the tremendous loss of my mother being diagnosed with Alzheimer's; my brother Dan being diagnosed with lung cancer; my niece by marriage dying an untimely death, leaving my nephew behind with an infant and a toddler; being thousands of dollars in debt; working three jobs or more; making terrible decisions financially, physically, and spiritually; and letting the important things pass me by. I was in a dark hole and had lost all confidence in my abilities. I was miserable. Even worse, I kept it all inside. I was totally and utterly alone. All the while, I kept the façade of being okay with everything. All of the messages I had heard in my life from those who had tried to control me and those messages I had given myself for years were all true: I was overwhelmed and believed I was broken, poor, unattractive, obese, stupid, not able to make good decisions, and not able to take care of myself. Being a single parent in my midforties with three very bright, beautiful, needy children was not where I wanted to be and not the kind of example I wanted to be for my children or anyone. Feeling seriously flawed and continually beating myself up for anything and everything, I was lost. I had surely fallen from grace with no way in sight to find the light—any light.

The evidence was stacked against me, and as they say in research, it was valid and reliable. No money, poor self-esteem, poor health, and no positive outcomes in sight. I was all alone, a feeling all too familiar, and suffering in my silence. Give, give, give was the word that went over and over in my mind and it was never, never, never enough, and, worse, I internalized it as I was never, never, never enough! My life had become drudgery; I would go home, go to bed, get up, go to work, go home, and back to work again. Being exhausted and overwhelmed, I wanted to hide with nowhere to go.

I had been through hard times before as a child, and my divorce was very difficult, my father's death was almost unbearable, and other circumstances had been really hard, but this period of my life was different. Before, I could put the focus on someone else or external influences causing my pain, and I would not feel the weight of the responsibility like half-ton boulders on my shoulders. This time, I knew much of it was my own doing and how I had developed from my own life experiences, and even worse, I knew *I* had to be the one to pull myself out of this hole. My addiction to perfection was not okay anymore. The pain of staying the same was greater than the pain of letting go and taking action.

From my profession, I knew that many in the field of addiction call this "hitting the bottom," and it certainly was the bottom for me, but I have treated many individuals addicted to substances and other things that never get to what they call the bottom, even after losing everything and everyone. Also, I've provided treatment for those that make changes way before getting to what they would define as "the bottom." The one thought I kept in mind is that it is different for everyone. For me, whatever it was—a light bulb moment, a revelation, or something else—it was above all profound and meaningful. Linda Sue McCall, this perfect woman, had fallen from grace and needed to find the light.

From my life experiences and from helping others by providing therapy, I knew the way to get beyond the circumstances, the crippling self-doubt, the toxic self-hatred, and the perfectionism:

I was to revisit my past, resolve my pain, and to write my new future.

And, I did.

Part II
Revisiting My Past

Chapter Six
Embrace Therapy

Growing up in poverty, my family and I never went to medical doctors when we were sick unless we were near death or had been in an accident. The first time I went to a dentist was at twelve years old, so therapy was not only out of the question, it was never even considered. I do not think I even knew what therapy was until my oldest sister developed a major mental illness the same year that I went to see the dentist for the first time. I believed I got more help from the dentist (and I so hated getting teeth filled and pulled) than she did from therapy.

Even at my age, I knew she was not getting better. This was my precious sister Jean; I loved her more than life, and she continued to disintegrate right before my eyes. I cried out to God, I cried out to the universe, I cried out to my mother to help, but my cries were not heard, or so it seemed. The Jean I knew was somehow leaving, and there was nothing I could do about it, and, worse, I did not understand it at all.

My parents took her to her appointments with her psychiatrist, but they did not know what to do outside of that; it seemed as if they did nothing, which was very typical. They did not know what was happening, and there was no help in sight from anywhere. The way

I managed this confusion at my age and in my own mind was to decide my sister could change back to her old self if she really wanted to; that was the only way I could make sense out of this senseless situation. For many years, I watched her go in and out of psychiatric hospitals being suicidal most of the time and at other times being totally out of control in various manic phases. I longed for her healing and her return to the person she was before mental illness. The loss was tremendous so to detach from her was survival for me. I, like my parents, did not know what to do and we were so isolated, proud, poor, and uninformed that we didn't know how to get help and certainly didn't want to ask for help from anyone.

As Jean went in and out of episodes, I believe she tried to reclaim herself. After her divorce, she went back to our home church and asked to teach Sunday school where she was once so active, and the deacons there told her she could not teach due to being divorced and that being against God's word. She went to work at a company ten miles away from home and worked there without missing a day and often not taking breaks, only to have an outburst once and be fired on the spot. With the powerlessness that was pervasive in our family, we continued to watch, knowing that this was not okay and that it should never happen to anyone and certainly not to anyone as precious as Jean.

Remembering back to earlier times before Jean's mental illness, our lives were filled with so many challenges. Emotions in our home were volatile and difficult to keep under wrap. There seemed to always be anger, conflict, and chaos, and little that was in the moment and present. But Jean was wonderful. She took care of the younger children much of the time, and I, being the youngest, received the majority of her care. Some of my fondest memories are of the many nights she would tiptoe, quiet as a mouse, sneaking ice cream to Joyce and me in bed way past our bedtimes. It was totally fine with us that she woke us up. Those nights were the best: eating that butter pecan ice cream and talking about our day and hers was wonderful and some of the sweetest memories.

As a teenager, Jean was a devoted Christian and rarely missed a church service. Her favorite scripture from the King James Version of the Bible was Psalm 23:

> The Lord is my shepherd; I shall not want. He maketh me to lie down in green pastures: he leadeth me beside the still waters. He restoreth my soul: He leadeth me in the paths of righteousness for his name's sake. Yea, though I walk through the valley of the shadow of death, I will fear no evil: for thou art with me; Thy rod and staff they comfort me. Thou preparest a table before me in the presence of mine enemies: thou anointest my head with oil; my cup runneth over. Surely goodness and mercy shall follow me all the days of my life: and I will dwell in the house of the Lord forever.

This beautiful Psalm was read at her funeral by her son a few short years ago, after pancreatic cancer took her life. These lovely words from the Bible carried Jean through some very dark times in childhood and in her teen years, but they weren't enough to prevent the debilitating mental illness that changed her in her early 20s and literally changed our lives forever. If you've never experienced a major mental illness with a loved one or yourself, I hope and pray that you do not. There is no way to describe the unresolved emotions; there is just a coming together day by day to do the best you can to get the most help and assistance you can find. Gratefully, some of the newer medications have helped tremendously. About eight years before Jean's death, she was placed on Clozaril, a medication that brought her back to our family in a very wonderful way. For those years, I am so very grateful, and writing for the rest of our family, I know they are grateful as well.

The impact

Due to my sister's illness and my father and brother's alcoholism, I had the desire to understand what had happened to them and had many unanswered questions. On some level, even though I didn't speak of it, I believe subconsciously I had some concerns that the same thing might happen to me. After receiving my two-year degree in criminal justice, I was drawn to psychology and social work when I made the decision to further my education; I learned the root causes of mental illnesses and addictions, and what therapy was and how it could, and did, help others. I immersed myself in self-help books and training, and I went to various self-help groups and even went to individual therapy a few times. Making the decision at that time, I decided that therapy was for others and not for me. Once I got it, the "it" being that I could benefit from therapy, I decided it was time to take the blinders off and find someone that could be beneficial to me.

The first time I really went to see a therapist and knew I would follow through, I was clear on exactly what I wanted. I remember that day as if it were yesterday, I walked into her office and said, "I want you to help me do one thing; I want to leave my husband." I made it clear that I really didn't care if she helped me to do anything else. I had decided that he was at the core of all my problems. My goal was to get out of the bad relationship that I blamed for much of the unhappiness in my life. Surprisingly, after a year with her, one to two times a month, I was finished with my marriage. The divorce came later, but psychologically for me, my marriage had ended, and I knew it was only a matter of time before I made the ultimate decision to leave. Remembering the first nine months in therapy, from the minute I walked into her office until I left, I cried tears that flowed like rivers. I cried about the loss of my dreams of pursuing beauty pageants and modeling and missing out on the career I could have had and the money I could have made. I cried about the feelings that I had from the man I married of never being good enough, thin enough, smart enough, etc., which reinforced my beliefs of myself. I cried for my children and for the dysfunctional relationship of this marriage and how I saw it impacting them. When the tears began to subside, I found direction and peace. The rivers of tears I had cried propelled me forward in slow, steady movements until I was firmly out to sea, heading in a new direction. Many thanks belongs to this wonderful therapist for being a bridge in my healing and in my life. The credit for having the courage to follow through and be consistent in my goal and actually make the changes is mine though. I did the homework to find the best therapist for me, which made the difference, and I had the willingness to do the work to get the help I needed. For all of us, we need to determine the best use of the money and time we have and what our priorities are. For me, what I gained from that year was priceless.

Following my divorce

With perfection still controlling my life, and my later fall from grace—with no one to blame and many circumstances outside of my control—I drew on my past experiences of therapy and found a different therapist that I believed could meet my needs. During the same time, I began embarking on new and different types of training to improve my ability to help others through providing therapy. I started attending trainings in a variety of therapies that up until then would not have been considered. It was good learning how to be a better therapist with more tools to use; but what was even better was when I would attend these trainings, and through the teachings, I would be a client as well as an observer and then a therapist—everyone taking the training had to do the same. In one of the trainings in particular, the instructor told us to process something that bothered us mildly but was not something that would cause a significant abreaction or be too hard for us to handle in a professional setting. Of course, being a perfectionist and going on two speeds most of my life—all or nothing—I went with the "ALL." I wanted the full benefit and did not want to waste my time. This particular training was on Eye Movement Desensitization and Reprocessing (EMDR); I chose two events in two different sessions—one was when I almost drowned sometime in the 1960s and the other was when I failed the fourth grade in elementary school. Each of these events had been quite traumatic in my childhood. To explain a little further about EMDR, it is a complex multiple-phase treatment that is highly utilized for individuals who have experienced traumatic events. As stated in some literature: "In successful EMDR therapy, the meaning of painful events is transformed on an emotional level."[1]

Basically, I was first taught how to relax on a deep level so that when upsetting thoughts came, I was able to relax. Then the therapist would ask me to come up with an issue that was upsetting to me, and he would get a gauge of how upsetting on a scale of one to ten, with ten being the highest level of being upset. He then would ask where I felt the feelings in my body—such as, if I had any pain or discomfort. I was then asked to choose a negative belief about myself related to the issue that upset me. The belief could be anything, but it needed to be specific. A typical belief for me at that time was I am unworthy, shameful, bad, etc. Then I would be asked to come up with a statement that is the opposite of the negative belief, such as I am worthy, good, etc. The positive statement would then be given a number to determine how much I believed the positive statement on a scale of one to six, with six being the highest. Then, a series of eye movements or hand taps would be initiated by the therapist—I could

---

[1] "What is EMDR?" *EMDR Institute, Inc.* http://www.emdr.com/general-information/what-is-emdr/what-is-emdr.html.

follow his hand from side to side with my eyes or he could tap my hands alternately while I began remembering upsetting events of my past. After each period, he would allow me to stop, take a deep breath, and talk about what I was experiencing. After several time periods, he would go back and process each one individually and have me visualize the event as if I was an observer and watching it on a movie. Then, while eye movements or hand taps are continuing, the therapist would guide me to stop watching the movie and walk outside and get in my vehicle and drive away, leaving it all in the past. He would then tell me to take a deep breath. This would continue as I processed events that triggered a reaction at different times of my life. It was automatic, and the events just kept coming. After completely processing all of the events, he would ask me to close my eyes and scan my body to find any pain, irritation, or discomfort that was left. Then he would do further hand taps or eye movements to resolve the discomfort if there was any. Lastly, he would ask me about the two levels earlier about how upset I was feeling at the end and how much I believe the positive statement given. With the initial numbers being different and significantly improved, I would leave the session with instruction to be aware of issues that surface afterwards and be prepared to process them in future sessions. Once the initial EMDR session occurs, it is not unusual for other issues to arise to address. I was encouraged to keep a record of those.

After the EMDR intervention/training, these events I had addressed had lost their power in my life. It is a tremendous therapy; when utilized by skilled therapists, the changes can be remarkable. I found out firsthand what could and did make the difference.

Finding a new therapist

I looked for someone who was nontraditional. I needed someone to teach me how to bulldoze the psychological house that I had built and how to build a new one that would be structurally safe and steadfast. The EMDR was helpful, and I wanted to know more about other therapeutic techniques. By this time, I had my master's degree in social work and was providing therapy and counseling services to many of my own clients. I had the luxury of knowing what many therapists knew about therapy and found one that was right for me. Mostly, this therapist challenged me, and the more I went to see her the more I wanted to learn. She had a charisma about her that few individuals, much less therapists, had and I wanted to have the same thing. She was certified in hypnotherapy and some other alternative therapies, and I was interested and willing to try it.

Growing up in the area known as the "Bible Belt," I was taught that therapists that do not teach strictly by the Bible are wrong and not helpful. It seems ridiculous, but there are many things I feared out of lack of knowledge. The one blessing at this time in my life was that the fear to try something new was less than the fear of staying the same. So I took the plunge, and it helped to change my life. My time seeing this therapist was not long, but she was a strong catalyst in my healing and helped me to find the light. I enrolled in the two-year internship program she had attended at the Wellness Institute in Issaquah, Washington. In the beginning, I was trained in meditation, heart-centered hypnotherapy, breath-release therapy, psychodrama, etc., and continued to be involved in the training of various therapeutic modalities for about three more years after I completed the internship program. Three to four times a year, I flew to where these trainings were provided. All individuals—mostly licensed therapists, psychologists, nurses, and medical doctors—receiving the training agreed to do their own work in the trainings, which consisted of being clients as well as therapists. The experience in hypnotherapy, breath-release therapy, and psychodrama/hypnodrama has not only made a significant difference in my life, but in the lives of many. Looking back, I think the greatest part of the healing was in being able to heal the subconscious mind—once that is done, we are no longer controlled by our impulses and our triggers from the past. I am grateful to the teachers of the Wellness Institute for the space they provided for me to gain these therapeutic tools. God has been good to place many bridges in my life, and at the Wellness Institute, there were many who used their talents and gifts to provide a place of healing from the past for those with the courage to do the work.

Meditation

The meditation consisted of guided meditation with music and scripts to follow. The focus was on clearing the various energy fields in the body and of protection from negativity. Since I had tried meditation multiple times with little to no success, it was great to finally find something that worked for me. I was able to relax on a very deep level and began to feel much clearer and better day to day. Letting go of the negativity was very powerful, and the most wonderful benefit of the meditation was being able to feel grounded after the meditations. By being grounded, I mean being present and fully aware of my feelings and of those around me, as well as aware of the events taking place. Much of my life until then had been lived in numbness and denial. The meditation helped by providing me with peace and tranquility.

Heart-Centered Hypnotherapy

Prior to taking the two-year internship at the Wellness Institute, I had taken a six-day course on hypnosis and learned some of the basic skills and was able to work towards certification. In this particular training, I was given scripts to follow that allow the client to get the feelings out of his/her body – even during the sessions, it was about knowing where the traumas, or painful events are stored in the body and how to yell them out or beat them out on a punching bag. The skills taught while in trance were experiential with activity instead of sitting or lying down while communicating the feelings. In the two-year internship, I learned more about how to do this on an intensive level and most importantly, it was in a safe place with therapists and others with similar experiences. Finding healing for me was more powerful with those who were skilled and likeminded. Finding healing for the inner child and helping her to heal at the various developmental stages helped me to grow and to become more the person I truly was instead of the façade of whom I had subscribed.

Psychodrama/Hypnodrama

Psychodrama is a very intensive group therapy. It is complex and involves the primary individual, often referred to as the protagonist, and many other roles of the other participants as it relates to the primary individual. Hypnodrama, as I understand it, is psychodrama while in a trance state. At the Wellness Institute, we learned and benefited from hypnodrama. We followed much of the same protocols as those do in psychodrama so that the scenes were as if they were occurring in the present, and the others in the psychodrama played different roles assigned by the protagonist. It was very experiential; individuals acted out how the situations were, and the protagonist was able to say what he/she wanted to say in the moment that he/she wanted to say it. It was like rewriting history but in a very healing/positive way. The result most often provided the individual observing or participating empowerment by taking power and renewing hope for lost events.

Breath-Release Therapy

Breath-release therapy has been around for many years, and it is very simple but powerful. It is a holistic technique that encourages balance of the body, mind, and spirit. It is increased breathing at a rapid pace for a long period (from forty-five minutes to two hours); it aids in releasing the negativity, freeing blockages and deep-seeded emotions of the past.

Amazingly, many miracles occurred during the time I was involved in this training and therapy. There was no way that I could afford the trainings and/or the therapy from my therapist. The therapist I found charged me $50.00 per session, and I had a supervisor at a part-time job that approved the costs for most of the trainings for EMDR and the Wellness Institute for the first three years. Also, the Wellness Institute provided a way that I could make payments until I was able to pay the remainder of the money I owed. Interesting how once I made the choice to heal and ask God for help in doing so, many miracles and possibilities appeared.

What I have learned

Unfortunately for many with perfection issues, if they develop a chronic mental illness, the recovery from perfectionism is not always as successful as quickly as for others. Medication coupled with psychotherapy can still make a big difference, but one has to ensure the person providing the treatment has significant expertise in trauma and mental illness, devises a highly specific and specialized individual plan and follows it, and ensures involvement of the medical community for the best results. Depending on the illness, symptoms, and behaviors there might not be the insight needed to find the relief desired through certain psychotherapies. Due to Jean's illness and the lack of services early on, she probably would not have benefited so much from the psychotherapy that has helped many to find the light.

Even so, she is definitely in the light now, and her loving spirit lives on through her family, children, grandchildren, and those of us who will always love her dearly. My sister and her mental illness had a profound impact on my life and were instrumental in my career choice as a therapist, a clinical social worker, and an advocate for those unable to speak out.

The reality is that one needs to get out of the darkness as soon as possible and be open to help from others. Had my sister gotten the help she needed as a child and a teenager prior to some traumatic events occurring in her 20s, would she have had the psychotic break that led to her major illness? Was it her hereditary predisposition to mental illness? Was it her upbringing in our dysfunctional family? Was it the traumatic events that occurred as an adult? Or was it something else or everything else? We will never know. Our family came to the place where we realized that there are no answers for many questions, there are just questions. Through many studies, it is difficult to ascertain what ultimately causes a psychotic break to occur, but there is much more that we know now about prevention and treatment. We never really know as therapists and social workers if we can change the path for someone before it is too late.

For many fortunate enough not to have a psychotic break or for those who recover from the psychosis, the road to healing and wellness can be embraced more quickly and fully. It's important to get beyond the judgments, prejudices, and stigma of the illnesses and of receiving help from a professional who knows how to provide treatment. I had to get through my own judgments because of my sister's illness and the lack of treatment for her, but whatever the issues are that keep one from trusting, it is important to just move through them.

My recommendation to others is to do the research and find the therapist and therapies that are right for you. If it is lack of money, time, etc., find a therapist who will work with you where you are—there are many professionals that work with individuals on a sliding fee scale or for free. Call the ones that you feel drawn to contact and talk with them about what you are seeking. Know what you want in your life to be different, whether you feel like you can change it or not, let the therapist guide you to finding the light. I know it does not work for everyone but it does work for many. If you have made the choice to try alternative therapies, find a therapist that has a special skill such as one of the ones I have mentioned in this chapter. It's okay if he or she doesn't have them all, even one of them can make a significant difference.

Chapter Seven
Become Educated

One key to my own freedom was to get a master's degree and be able to find a job and be able to support myself and my family. For many, they can go back to school or learn a skill to become independent thinkers. At times when I would have difficulty with understanding something, I would do research and read as much as possible. It helped me to find out what others had done before me and helped me to be open-minded and able to see other possibilities. My father was not able to do so.

"My father was not an educated man." Of course, there is no shame in that statement, but this is one of the statements I have used all my life. Now, I'll be real honest and inform you that my father was not educated at all—he was illiterate. He could not read or write. Recalling from my youth, he would tell the story to my siblings and me of quitting school in the second grade and having to work to support his family. After hearing the story of quitting school at such a young age and of the many hardships he experienced, we felt so sorry for him that we never questioned him further as to why he was illiterate. When he would tell this story, he would firmly state that all of his children would finish high school. Anything less would be unacceptable. There were nine children in his family of origin, and only one of the nine graduated from high school. All of my siblings and I graduated from high school. He would have had it no other way.

From a very young age, I sincerely believed that none of my siblings and I would ever go to college. People who went to college were smart, came from wealthy families, and had money. We didn't have money or smarts, and I saw no way that we could overcome the obstacles. To complicate my feelings of inadequacy in education, having failed the fourth grade, I believed that I might not even be able to finish high school. Surely, not passing a grade would be the strongest indicator that I would never go to college and that I would never make it.

I digress, but failing the fourth grade was embarrassing; the shame was almost unbearable and I had to face it for years. I, at that time, so wanted to run away and hide. But, being the tallest girl in the class, which magnified my feelings, I soaked up the embarrassment and shame with nowhere to hide. The way I dealt with the pain was to blame it on my teacher, and the reality is that it was partially her fault; she told my mother and I that if I significantly improved my grades the last nine weeks that I would be promoted to the fifth grade. I did that and it still wasn't enough—that teacher was just one more in a long list of individuals teaching me that I should strive for perfection. On top of all that, I did not even like school. I didn't like the homework, and I didn't like having to write thousands of sentences a week: "I must not talk in class." I think if I had a dollar for every time I wrote that sentence or every time my hand got slapped by a ruler, I'd be wealthy; in fact, there is no question in my mind that I would be a rich woman. Writing this now, I understand why she might not have promoted me to the fifth grade; it must have been hard for her to teach with me in her class, but I had somehow thought that teachers were true to their word.

No matter how bad school was or what happened during the day, I always knew someone would be waiting for me. My sister

Joyce, who was two years older, always saved a seat just for me on the big yellow school bus that took us up the mountain to God's Country. Knowing that she was there for me was very special, and I knew everything would be okay once I sat down beside her—and it was.

I told Joyce, as I did everyone in my family, that I would make up the year that I spent repeating the fourth grade. For years, I informed my family and friends that I would finish high school in three years and later was true to my word. I graduated with my class, and I fulfilled that goal in my life.

My brother Royce, who is also two years older than me and is Joyce's twin, had a dream to go to college, and not just any college; he wanted to go to Clemson University. Such as this was never heard of in my family—either we went to trade schools or technical schools, but never to Clemson. Royce was an inspiration; if he did it, I wanted to do it. I remember well the night when he came home after church when a married couple there had offered to pay his college tuition. The twinkle in his eyes was the same bright light I saw but few times on special occasions; it was a Santa Claus moment when he received something so great that there were no words big enough to express the feelings. Seeing the excitement in his eyes was priceless. He had studied hard and had made the grades to get into Clemson University, never knowing how he would ever be able to pay for it, and his prayers were answered.

Royce was a tremendous role model for me in my education; he loved to learn and loved to read and study. He had confidence that he could make it through college and he did. My admiration for my brother Royce runs deep. He was a sensitive man who listened and understood feelings, which was different from many others in the family. It never really mattered to him whether or not he was an alpha male. Even though he never said it, it was clear that he did not want to be like our father. He never fell into the same patterns of some of the others in the family. He was not into smoking or drinking. He was and is a different kind of man, and was with me through some of my most difficult years and offered, through his example, many gifts, especially the gifts of learning and education.

Now, when we are at a family gathering and we say the usual good-byes and I-love-yous, he always says, "I'm glad you got to see me," and, with that same laughter and wonderful twinkle in his eyes and a hug of pure love, I have a Santa Claus moment—I am grateful.

What I have learned

When the acknowledgment that the end of a journey is near and one finds himself or herself in the trenches, the very energy it takes to move forward seems nonexistent. Some of my clients have been unable to get out of bed in the morning, much less actually work on getting better. What often makes the difference for some is in how long they stay stationary and when staying stuck is more painful than doing something about it. Many of my clients express that they cannot crawl out of the hole where they find themselves. Some actually stay in the hole for a while. To some, I am able to say that when they stay in the hole, they are making a decision to do so. Others can't hear such a thing; then my training and my love for them kicks in, and I just meet them where they are until they build a firm foundation under their feet. Mostly when I work with clients that have a great deal of insight, they have either grown up in a home of highly intelligent people or they are educated or they read and learn as much as possible. This is certainly not true in all cases; some individuals have poor insight with lots of education, even with a family with lots of education, and some the opposite. The point here is that everyone is different; no two individuals are the same, and we all have different goals and aspirations and different wants and needs. With the individuals with perfectionist traits that I have assisted in healing, the ones with the best outcomes tend to be the ones who want to learn everything they can possibly learn and apply that knowledge in order to find healing, health, and wellness.

What I encourage my clients to do is to draw from their past accomplishments and gain strength from what has helped them to be successful in the past. One area that I have them focus on is that of learning as much as possible. I've heard it stated that awareness is the precursor to change, and I do agree. To take it one step further, knowledge is the precursor to lasting change. If we are not knowledgeable, we do not know what we do not know. Please don't miss this: ignorance is not bliss; ignorance is bondage. It is important to make sense of how we got to where we are in order to be able to go in a different direction. The importance of gaining knowledge cannot be stressed enough. When we are knowledgeable, we know that we have choices. Whether we make the choices that are best for us or not is totally up to us and where we are in our journeys. My education gave me freedom, and that made the difference.

Chapter Eight
Be Clear in Religion/Spirituality

The King James Version was the only Bible available to me back in the 1960s through the first part of the 1970s; we would read and study it and try to make sense of the strange wording and phrasing, but it was difficult. My parents didn't go to church but perhaps for a few times that I recall. My father and mother were both religious in some respects: my dad never worked on Sunday, which was biblical, and my mother quoted the Bible many, many, many times. I wonder if I wrote "many" enough to give her the credit she deserves. Anyways, Mom knew the Bible and she believed it. She made sure that if any of us wanted to go to church that we had transportation to go by one of the neighbors since she didn't drive. I remember my dad dropping us off from time to time, but he did not stay at the church with us. I remember one of the times my mother went to church with us, and I was somewhere around five or six years old. I was being disrespectful and stuck my tongue out at her. Before I had a moment to realize what was happening, she picked me up out of the church pew, took me outside of the church, found a hickory stick (branch from a nearby bush/tree), and the rest is history. My parents believed in corporal punishment, "spare the rod, spoil the child," but there were alternatives and they just didn't know or understand them. They knew that spanking was quick and effective. In a poverty-stricken home, it is understandable, but from my perspective, it was not necessary.

When I had fallen from grace, I went back to my roots and explored my childhood decisions about God. It became evident to me that I did not know God. On many levels, not only did I not know God, I was angry with the God I thought I knew.

Early decisions about God as far back as I can remember were based on fear, shame, and guilt, and yet many talked of God's love and I did not understand the connection. The ministers and deacons in the church were all men, and I had such fear around men and kept my distance from all of them. Women taught Sunday School and led the choir, but weren't allowed to pray out loud in the church services. "Women had their place." The men, on the other hand, had their place as well, but it always seemed far superior to the women.

In our small country church, we had several ministers that were very good and kind, but many were driven by how many individuals they "saved," which is okay in some respects. From my perspective, when it was negative, it was from their egos and a religious/spiritual bypass; they had no idea how their egos and unfinished/unresolved issues of their past bled over into their messages. The way I see it, spiritual bypass for influential leaders is like an artist who has painted a picture and it is bleeding through the lines. One example of this is a tactic that many Southern Baptist ministers use even to this day: they will have singing after their preaching services to bring those in the congregation to be saved. Many times, prior to the singing, in prayer, the minister would ask those in the congregation to raise their hands if they felt led by the Holy Spirit to be saved or to rededicate their lives to Christ; he would remind the congregation that everyone else had their eyes closed. Then the singing would begin and all those who had raised their hand were pressured by the minister to come to the front of the church. Since they had felt the calling of God, they were to come to be saved. Knowing that the minister saw the hands that were raised, many go to the front of the church and "accept Christ as their personal savior" without really knowing or understanding what that means and the responsibility of such. I know—I was one who went up several times.

Early in my childhood, my mother told the story many times of a preacher who used this tactic and kept the whole church singing long after the service to save my dad. Once my father had attended and walked out of the church, and the preacher even followed him out of the church to get him to repent and be "saved." Of course, the whole congregation witnessed it; my dad went to church rarely and resisted going to any church at any time afterwards. Even now, I fail to see how embarrassment and shame brings anyone to the love of God. It was a violation of trust regardless of how unintended. To me, that is opposite of the love and forgiveness that Jesus taught and preached. Unfortunately, living in a small rural community, everyone at this church knew my dad, and he knew, firsthand, how many of them lived their lives. My father was an all or nothing kind of man; I believe that had he become a Christian, he would have been a good one, all the way.

Several years later, a man preached at the church where I was a member and then decided to take on the job as minister. The committee hired him as a full-time minister; many in my family and in the community were hopeful that this preacher would be a change agent in our small community. With this preacher, the church attendance tripled, and we were "on fire for Christ," or so that was the saying. One of my dad's brothers became a born-again Christian and gave up alcohol, and our family was hopeful that my father would be next. Unfortunately, some things happened to rock our faith. The main situation that occurred was that the preacher left the church and his wife to have an affair with another woman in the church; in a small community, it quickly became common knowledge. Not surprisingly, most of that was pinned on the other woman, but the minister resigned from the church as a result of that affair. The people of the community were devastated, but many in my family were heartbroken; we had lost hope for my dad and his salvation, which we believed was our only hope for change in his life and ours.

My fathers' salvation in the Southern Baptist church never came before his passing from this life, as far as we know; no one knows for sure if it happened or not before his death. My uncle's salvation did, and his life was very different. Many years later, my oldest brother, Dan, became a Christian and changed his life. The changes in their lives were examples that I would have never wanted to miss, and I am so grateful to God for the transformations in their lives. To witness the two of them living many years of their lives as wonderful, loving Christian men was a great blessing to me and to others. Free of alcohol, negativity, and darkness, they were two of the finest men I have ever known, and the impact of their lives continues to influence those who knew them.

My personal beliefs

There were several times when I thought I had found God. I have been baptized twice and rededicated my life to Christ many times, but I never really felt the totality of God's love until I released my thoughts of religion and my beliefs of who and what I believed about God.

Many times religious leaders, Christians, spiritual leaders, counselors, and therapists get caught up in their egos and spiritual judgments and beliefs, and they haven't dealt with their own issues of shaming, judging, and criticizing others. Not being present, they are unaware of how their past influences their present emotions and relationships. This type of bypass keeps them stuck and unable to truly help others due to their lack of insight and authenticity.

Once I worked through my own spiritual bypass and was able to let go of judgments and legalism, I found a relationship with God. No longer am I afraid of God even though I give him ultimate respect. He is a living God and is available. The most wonderful and powerful parts of having a relationship with God is not feeling alone. In my life, when I truly found God, I found peace and I found myself. I released judgments about others, and myself and I found a way to forgive those that I felt had wronged me and forgive myself for areas in which I felt damaged. I found prayers and beliefs that kept me strong and helped me to help others. I released the darkness and negative thoughts of others and myself and began a life of light and fulfillment. I released sadness and self-hatred. I found love for others and myself where ever we were on our journeys. And, I make every day and sometimes every moment count. Living in the moment and loving myself, I found a real and living God. The God I serve is a God that I feel with me all the time, not a God that I serve, sense, or visit on Sundays and Wednesday nights at church. To me, God is everywhere and in everything he supplies to give us life. When I don't feel his presence, I have songs in my heart and sayings in my mind that will bring him close to me.

There are many songs I love—"Amazing Grace," is one of those. Many other songs, especially Christian hymns, bring me closer to God when difficulties arise.

Other songs that are not as traditional are songs that I learned at various trainings and workshops, and I integrate them into my life at times when I need to feel the presence of a higher power. There is a song that I sing silently when I am with my clients and I feel they need God's love as much as I do, and it is a song I learned at the Wellness Institute during a weekend of training. It is a Native American song we sang repeatedly as we were preparing for a fire walk to face our fears:

> Oh Great Spirit, Earth and Sky and Sea, You are inside,
> And all around me.

As I sing it over and over in my mind, the air in the room seems to change, and a feeling of peace and calm moves away all discord. It is the same peace that I felt as I walked over the hot coals in Issaquah, Washington, several years ago.

It is not unusual for me to be in a grocery store, on my front porch, or in my car and see the sun as a beautiful, brilliant light coming into my awareness and my life. As I am in the sunlight and I feel the presence of God, I pray:

> You who are the source of all power...whose rays illuminate the world...illuminate my heart also, so that it too may do your work, Amen.

When I am feeling down about a situation, I remind myself of positive affirmations (I have many) that are a part of my life through my healing and finding the light. An example is:

> Easily and Effortlessly, I call on God always.
> God is with me and I am safe, guided, loved, and protected.
> I am worthy and precious.

Another prayer that I have recently added in my silence when I desire to feel God's presence is part of the Prayer of Peace of Saint Francis of Assisi, which I have heard many times in the past but it was recently given to me by a special friend:

> Lord, make me an instrument of your peace;
> Where there is hatred, let me sow love;
> Where there is injury, pardon;
> Where there is discord, harmony;
> Where there is error, truth;

Where there is doubt, faith;
Where there is despair, hope;
Where there is darkness, light;
And where there is sadness, joy . . .

Throughout the many hardships in my life, I went through times of being angry with God and questioning him and even questioning his existence, but when I truly found God, I did discover who I was. It was only then that my life—the difficulties and the blessings—made sense.

Now, when I wake in the mornings and I hear the songs of the beautiful birds outside of my bedroom window, I feel the love of God. When I hear the purring of my sweet cats, I feel God's love. When my sweet dogs lick my face and wag their tails, I feel the love of God, and I know beyond a shadow of doubt that God is real and that I am loved, guided, protected, and safe.

What I have learned

What I see as the best way to move forward is to be working on the relationship with oneself and God (however you see God) simultaneously. If one is not clear on what the issues are or how to start, ask God, your higher power, or the Angels to help you to find clarity. Then seek help from others who have found the love that you want to have—for me, God is synonymous with love. Many of my clients have come to me over the years broken, devastated, and wounded by religion, religious leaders, spirituality, and spiritual leaders. It's not that they had necessarily been abused by them or attacked, even though that certainly has happened with some. For many, the ministers and leaders in the religious/spiritual community were not there for them at critical times or the person asking for help was blamed in some way for what happened to them. Sometimes, the issue was that the leaders did nothing at all and certainly nothing to help. Many believed that since God was not there for them in their deepest time of pain that he was not a reliable God and anything positive heard or read about God was not true.

Others endured spiritual abuse in relationships with a relative or partner where they were controlled by their faith and the manipulation of others using their faith. Many caught up in abusive relationships quote the Bible to control others—how one can start to know that they are being abused is from the messages they get from their bodies. Over the years, I have had many women come to me for counseling that tell stories of not being able to say no to sex, not being able to speak their minds, of having to apologize for things (multiple times) that they do not believe are wrong, and of always having to be ruled and controlled by their husbands/partners. Their underlying belief expressed is that if I am just good enough (perfect enough), I will be loved by my husband/partner and I will be loved by God. The spiritual bypass for them is that they have combined God with their husbands/partners and are unable to separate the two. Their bodies are screaming at them for help, to be rescued from the stress, the pain, the disease(s), or the multiple physical disorders brought on by their stress, and they are not listening. Or, if they are, they don't know what to do about it.

What I have found as the key to helping them in finding the light is to help them to find love for themselves. Then they can begin to seek God (however they see God) through love, real love, and being present, which in turn is the opposite of caught up in spiritual bypass.

Spiritual bypass is something that many don't take seriously enough and is definitely a treatment issue. Often, individuals don't see themselves clearly because they have responses to situations that they have taken from the Bible or other spiritual texts and are thus unaware of how their own issues are clouding the meaning and understanding. Some authors and teachers are calling spiritual bypass "dissociation" and that may be as good of a definition as any. John

Welwood wrote about spiritual bypassing and defined it as he saw it in the Buddhist Community: "There being a tendency to use spiritual ideas and practices to sidestep or avoid facing unresolved emotional issues, psychological wounds, and unfinished developmental tasks." It is evident in so many ways and changes as we are able to verbalize our pain and move forward through healing. Through awareness, insight, and releasing judgments, many are able to discover for themselves how spiritual bypass has separated them from their true purpose and their joy.

Chapter Nine
Make Peace with Losses

Loss. The mere word causes a chill to run up my spine. When I lost my father in February of 1984, I felt like my heart was being ripped apart. The pain in my chest and stomach was a tremendous physical pain that I had never, ever felt before. Also, I was two months pregnant with my second child, and it was one of the few times in my life that I had no appetite and no way to stuff the pain. The night before and the morning of his death, I remember having gnawing feelings that I needed to call my father several times, but I had dismissed the feelings.

The weekend before his death, I had wanted to attend a family gathering but had not gone to visit. The visit was prohibited by the man I was married to at the time, who I refer to as X. He informed me I couldn't travel to South Carolina because we still owed money on a $1500 refrigerator we had recently purchased. If not before, at that point in time, I hated that refrigerator—a $500 refrigerator would have been fine for me. I guess hating an inanimate object was easier than hating the man I was married to and who was the father of my children.

My dad's passing was a shock. He had a massive heart attack after getting home from a fishing trip he had taken that morning with one of my nephews. He had been drinking the night before, and as he did so often after drinking, he stopped cold turkey the following morning. Later, I put together in my mind that the withdrawal from the alcohol and the physical exertion was too much, and his heart was unable to handle the intensity. His health had been declining for some time.

As it was conveyed to me, it was one of my niece's birthdays, and she walked into the house to visit and found him lying on the floor. She yelled for my mother, who quickly ran in from another room and tried to dissolve one of Dad's nitroglycerin tablets under his tongue; her attempt was unsuccessful, and even with emergency paramedics arriving at the home, he died. No one but my mother believed that his death could have been prevented that day. My mom was so angry with herself because she didn't put a nitroglycerin patch on his chest, but I guessed she was in such shock that she didn't even think of the patch. My mom was so caught up in her own issues with perfections that she was always blaming herself for something, and seeing herself as being responsible for dad's death was huge.

The emptiness we all felt was irreparable. My father had left us with so much unfinished business and so much baggage of words that were never said and feelings that were never expressed that we all left his funeral clinging onto every positive word that he had ever uttered to us; unfortunately, those words were few. Sadly, what made his death even more difficult to me were the beautiful stories told and heard from others about his goodness and help and his love for his family and the community. To hear his extended family members and the neighbors tell it, my father could have walked on water, and for them, it sounded like he did. He helped the needy, he put out fires, he never said "no" to requests for help, and the list of what he did for others went on and on. From rescuing dogs and cattle, to pulling vehicles out of ditches, to helping stop forest fires from spreading, he was always there and available. My father was a wonderful man in many respects, but with the people who needed him the most, he was physically and emotionally unavailable.

When it finally hit me that he was gone and would not be coming back, I was lost—a feeling all too familiar but magnified several hundred percent. Years later, I realized that what connected me so much to my father was that I was on a mission to earn his love through perfection. My internal interpretation of his love was that he would love me if I was good enough, right enough, just anything enough. I realized that feeling his love was based on my performance and what I could and should do, not unconditional love; it's not that he didn't want to love unconditionally, he just did not know how. Once this made sense to me, I was able to find peace with his passing and truly find myself minus the feeling of needing to please another to earn love. When I found myself, I found freedom. One of the greatest contradictions of life is the one I experienced from losing my father: "Out of the darkest of times we can find the brightest of lights."

During the time I am writing this book, my mother has been suffering from Alzheimer's disease, and she doesn't even recognize me. She was diagnosed with this disease right about the same time I experienced what I call "my fall from grace," which certainly had an impact on the depth of my sadness and my feelings of being overwhelmed and alone. To lose my mother has been a somber process. I think this is one area where God is sparing me the pain of dealing with losing her all at one time, unlike the shock of my father's death. It has been very gradual, very painful, and very lonely. She has been the one person who was always interested in what I had to say and how I was doing. My mother knows my heart and knows most everything about me like no one else. She used to call me every week and send me cards when I didn't visit for a while. Then it occurred to me that the calls and the cards were coming less and less, and then the calls and cards came no more.

I love my mother very much. Her gifts of love, kindness, compassion, and strength are unmatched by anyone. Perhaps, she projected her dreams onto me, and I'm not only okay with that, I am very grateful. One statement she told me more times than any other is that "You can do anything;" she saw that in me when I didn't see it in myself. Perhaps she saw it in me because she didn't see it in herself. She gave me this tremendously powerful message to carry me through the hard times. She would quote from the Bible the verse about having faith of a mustard seed to move mountains. The power in those statements has stuck like glue with me throughout the years and has brought me to the light no matter how far I stray from my path. As I continue to fulfill my destiny, I draw strength from her and her love throughout the years. Her love is a love so deep that it continues throughout her illness and will continue through me and all of the lives she has touched.

Loss of my siblings

Two of my siblings have passed away from cancer—Jean lived six months after her diagnosis and Dan lived six years after his. They were my oldest sister and oldest brother. In our large family, they were much like a second set of parents to us due to having so much responsibility for the family early on. I still miss them, and I draw strength from the love that was given to me from them. When hard times come, I remember back to the good times when they were here.

Loss of my animals

I realized the magnitude of my emotional connection with one of my dogs some time back when I was leaving to take her to the veterinarian to have her put to sleep. She had been ill for quite some time and had lost control of her bladder. Her arthritis had gotten so severe that she could no longer walk without tripping, and after several months of watching her decline, I made the difficult decision to let her go. She was a part of the family for about sixteen years. I believe I was in shock, and as I was backing out of my driveway, I ran into the fence in the front yard with my car, which is something I'd never done before. I have seen and heard of individuals having accidents when the stress and sadness of loss is significant. I believe due to my pain at the time and not being present that

I was prone to this accident, but it helped put into perspective how very difficult this was.

She was a black Labrador retriever—my daughter's dog—and I had rescued her from the animal shelter as a puppy. She was given the name of Donut because her stomach was so big when she was adopted; we found out later that her stomach was big due to parasites, not food. I had lost a cat of seventeen years a couple of years previous to Donut and lost a twelve-year-old cat four months after.

Two of my pets died untimely deaths when I was in another state on a trip one summer, and I believe those were some of the most difficult for me to release due to the feeling of responsibility for their loss. Even though I was hundreds of miles away, and I know intellectually I was not available to protect them, I blamed myself. My mother used to say "Time heals all wounds," and, even though I don't completely agree with that statement, I do believe that we can release the past and have peace with losses. The unconditional love given to us by our pets is a tremendous loss when they pass away.

It is the love that we have for and from the ones that have gone on before us that is key in moving forward and coming to terms with loss, but the ultimate importance is in finding self-forgiveness for those times that we need to release.

What I have learned

My clients are impacted by pain from many losses in their lives. The losses of loved ones, including partners, children, friends, family, colleagues, co-workers, and others, leave wounds in their hearts that remain open for many years if not for the rest of their lives. There is another type of loss that is often just as difficult, if not more, it comes from trauma, abuse, and situations beyond our control and situations in which we made decisions we regret and have impact in our loss. Some of my clients have come to me to find peace from significant losses in their lives. Since everyone experiences loss differently, it's important to take each client's issues for what they are and help them to develop a sense of how to resolve the feelings around the losses. I join them in their journey to find peace from whatever is tormenting them. Being the bridge for my calling and dealing with my own issues that may not make sense to many, I help them to find ways to heal the open wounds of their hearts, filling the holes of pain so that the scar tissue is all that is left.

Being in the counseling/therapy field for many years, I have been able to gain an understanding of loss and how to process it. I have seen and worked with many who should have died due to accidents and suicide attempts. In fact, there are many who have endured physical injuries that should have ended their lives—from jumping off bridges, to wrecking cars, to gunshots, to overdosing on pills—there is no way they should have survived, but surprisingly, they did. Then I have seen many die of what most of us would consider minor injuries or accidents or physical issues. What always comes to me now is that "it was his/her time," or, "it was meant to be." It doesn't make sense, but it was supposed to happen or it wouldn't have. It also brings me back to releasing it to God and the inner knowing that he is in control.

Accepting that God is in control so that anytime we experience loss, whether it is a death or loss in any other way, it is important to process the feelings and to give ourselves the time needed to process before moving forward. If not, the feelings will continue to resurface. Depending on the depth of the loss, some are easier to release than others. It is important to give ourselves the time needed to take care of our needs and to release the pain.

Chapter Ten
Release the Toxicity

In being able to find the light, I knew I had to process and release my past. I went back to several very painful times in my childhood with the lived experiences that kept me in bondage. Knowing that to move forward, I had to rid myself of the pain, and I needed to revisit and process the feelings that continued to be present and impact my relationships with those I love. Through my experiences, I discovered how one internalizes toxicity and how to release it, but I had to revisit it first.

The way I define toxicity is anything that is damaging to us and creates self-doubt and self-negativity at the core of our being. Often the individuals saying or doing things that impact us are not even aware of the effect, but that is their issue and ours to own. My mother used to tell the story of my birth, and you would just have to know my family to appreciate how she told the story to the fullest, but even my telling of how she told the story will help you to get an idea of how and when my path to perfection began and what I needed to release.

Mom

The story she would tell of my birth always included a great deal of drama. First, she would talk of how hard her pregnancy was with me and how much weight she had gained, and then she would go into detail about how painful her "dry birth" was and how it was one of the most painful experiences of her life. Evidently, her water had broken many hours prior to delivery. She would then add information about my birth weight being over ten pounds, which certainly added to the pain. She would tell this story over and over again to anyone and everyone who would listen.

The reason this story is so pivotal and so significant in my life is that I took it on. By that I mean I felt responsible for her pain. It was not logical and is not logical—most things we take on at early ages are not—but the fact remains that I loved my mother so much that to be responsible for a pain so great gave me the desire to do everything in my power to never allow myself to cause her pain again. I held onto this toxic belief for many years. It wasn't until I processed it at a weekend training at the Wellness Institute that I was able to release it.

Dad

In our family, my father was a very powerful man. It may have been his size and strength or could have been that he appeared to have no fear. It might even have been due to his alcoholism or just in the way that he walked or looked at his children with firmness. It could be his corporal punishment with his rough, calloused hands— he did hard manual labor from sunup to sundown. More than anything else, it was probably due to his inconsistency; we never knew what to expect from our dad. Regardless of the reason, my siblings and I feared him. He loved children and loved to show us off when we were very young. When I was around four or five years old, I remember my father would take me everywhere with him. At that time, I believed

I was his favorite child, and it never occurred to me that I was his favorite due to my age.

My mother, on the other hand, was very close to my heart in a different way from my dad. She loved to cook and would allow me to stand in a chair beside her and help her cook as far back as I can remember; those were some of the most special times of my childhood. She had difficulty setting boundaries and almost never said no to anyone about anything. The only times she said no were when external forces wouldn't allow it or perhaps she could blame it on my dad saying, "It will make your father mad." Otherwise, she tried to please everyone at all times, which, of course, is impossible. My mother was caught up in her own perfection. My mother had sadness about her all the time even though she might be smiling, and she would often stare off into space. She would say things to me like I was the most special person in the world to her.

A painful, profound experience I remember at the age of four or five was late in the day on a Saturday and my father was leaving to go down to the country store that was about a mile from our house. I asked if I could join him and he said yes, as he always did. On that trip, he made a stop at a man's house that sold moonshine. I remember him telling me not to tell my mother that he stopped there and I agreed that I wouldn't tell. Then I remembered how upset my mother got the last time he stopped there. Evidently, when my father would drink moonshine, he would get very sick. I realize now that it must have been lead poisoning, but at that time, I had no idea.

When my father and I returned home, I told my mother but asked her not to tell my Dad that I told. In that split second, I thought I saw fire in my mother's eyes. She immediately walked into the other room with me and confronted my father. When he asked who told her, she said, "Linda." At that time, any other name would have been better. My father looked at me with the same blazing red eyes as my mother and said, "I'll never take you anywhere else alone with me ever again." Unfortunately, he was a man who mostly kept his word.

These experiences plus others pushed the toxicity deeper into not feeling safe, being unable to trust anyone, and fearing that if I spoke up there was sure to be abandonment. I did not know at the time that sometimes adults have their own agendas and one can be caught in the middle of triangulations and then it becomes your (the third person's) fault.

Another episode

My father would often drink too much on weekends and would have angry tirades. I remember one of those times when I was in elementary school, he was furious at the younger children for playing on top of his newly purchased 1955 Chevrolet with our shoes on and leaving scratches. In his anger, he found a branch from a tree and started beating the three younger children with it; I remember thinking and feeling that we were all going to die. He started with my brother Royce, who got it the worst. My memories take me back to the screaming, the crying, and the yelling for help to stop my father, but it was useless. All six of us were crying and screaming for my dad to stop but to no avail. My mother got involved and gave him a smaller branch to hit us with, but he just became angrier and hit us harder. Then she finally stopped him; I remember my mother saying to him that he would never hit us again, and I do not think he did afterwards. That time was more than enough; it was so horrific that I blocked it out of my memory until my midforties. In a therapy training at the Wellness Institute, I remembered this and I revisited this situation numerous times. I went back to this situation at times, and the pain was so intense that I just continued to work through it. It took time, but now I can remember it, speak of it, and not immediately have a reaction. The toxicity I took on was that adults, especially men, are unpredictable and scary, and that parents are not to be trusted.

Another time

In my childhood, sometime around the age of six, I unleashed some of my anger that resulted in causing some pain to my brother Dan, who was nine years older than me. As you know by now, my upbringing was in a small rural southern farm where my siblings and I had many chores. My oldest siblings had the majority of the responsibilities, with my oldest brother being responsible for milking the cows, feeding the pigs, and ensuring the garden was kept up. Also, we had wood heat, and he made sure the wood was chopped and ready to burn in our wood heater.

Dan and I had a conflictual relationship to say the least. He was a very handsome young man with perfect teeth, red hair, and freckles. He was a good communicator and liked by most everyone. He worked hard. Few teenagers did the amount of work he did without complaining. He stayed up late at night, got up early to go to school, and built the fire in the wood stove before the rest of us got up. When it concerned me as a young child, I never got the sense that he liked me very much. I guess looking back, I was much more of an irritant to him than anything else. At that time, I probably didn't like him much either.

One of Dan's pastimes when I was age four or five was to take the head off my baby doll, Jackie Boy, and play baseball with it. From being hit with a bat many times, Jackie Boy had dents in his little plastic face and head, and his eyeballs were pathetic—one eye looked up and the other to the side. I still loved Jackie Boy dearly, but my memories take me back to a time of sadness when I would look at Jackie Boy's face. I couldn't understand why my brother wouldn't listen to me when I cried and told him not to hurt my baby doll. The powerlessness was pervasive, and I was always mad at him for how he treated Jackie Boy and me.

There was one particular day in which the events of our lives shifted. Dan was milking the cows, and I, as usual, asked him if I could go with him to feed the pigs. The pigs were down in a hollow in the back of the barn, and I had been forbidden to go there without supervision. After he said no several times, he proceeded to squirt milk on my cat and me and then left laughing to go down to the bottom of the hill.

The memories of that day are so vivid that it seems as if it were yesterday. Something came over me, and I decided to get even. I was at my limit and enough was enough! Watching until he got out of sight, I glanced onto the woodpile and noticed my brother's high school letter jacket. It was a beautiful jacket with the colors of purple and white and had a large purple "W" on the front. He loved it and had saved money for months to be able to purchase it from the school. Not realizing the depth of my actions and how they would impact my brother, with all the strength I could muster, I picked up the sharp, heavy ax and chopped his jacket to shreds. Later I discovered that my father had just sharpened the ax and that's probably the reason it cut so well.

Once I had chopped enough, I realized that I just might be in trouble. Afraid of the likely consequences, I quickly put the ax down, ran into the house, and hid under my bed. With my heart pounding so loudly I could hear it beating, I listened as I heard the screams and the cries from Dan. He was devastated, and the sounds seemed to go on forever.

My mother then called my name and said that if I didn't come out from hiding the punishment would be much worse. I should not have believed her; it was bad. The physical punishment was bad, but the emotional pain I felt inside for the pain I had inflicted on my brother was much worse. At that point in time, I decided that to inflict pain on someone else was not something I was the least bit interested in doing again. Sadly, he never had the money to buy another jacket. The toxicity I took on was that it was okay for me to hurt but not okay for me to hurt others.

It wasn't until sometime around 2005 or 2006 that I replaced his letter jacket. My therapist at that time had mentioned to me that I might want to replace it—that was something I had not thought of myself. From a place of love, I did replace this letter jacket and took a trip to South Carolina just to give it to him.

Looking back, for many years after Dan had finished high school he was an active alcoholic, and his alcoholism worsened when he was in the Army; I kept my distance from him. Later he gave it up and never drank alcohol again. I've heard it said and I have been taught that people cannot recover from alcoholism, but I do believe their lives can be completely transformed. My brother was clean and sober for probably twenty years before his death in 2012 and was an example of this transformation. He became a Christian and a great one. He was not judgmental, and he loved his family and friends with the love that could only come from a supernatural presence being with him.

Another blessing from difficulties is that miracles are everywhere. We can choose to be mindful for when they come and be aware to be thankful. I am so thankful for my brother's love and the many years I was able to get to know him—truly know him.

Resolving the toxicity

The most effective way to address toxicity for me was to revisit my past and "get it out of my body." I cried it out, yelled it out, wrote it out, beat it out on a punching bag, breathed it out, talked it out, exercised it out, and prayed and meditated it out. Alternative and experiential therapies were the key for me: EMDR, breath-release therapy, hypnotherapy, and psychodrama/hypnodrama were some of the therapies that helped me to resolve the pain of my past and move away from the poison that held me in bondage.

These processes may not be the best for everyone, and it could be that the thought of alternative therapies bring up unresolved fears in others. Certainly, other therapies such as cognitive behavioral therapy are evidenced-based and effective. Mindfulness is also very effective, and mindfulness is not new—it is thousands of years old. Whatever the issues are and whatever choices one might make is up to him/her and it is important to take the time, do the research, find out what is best, and actively work towards better health. It is worth the effort, time, and money. It can be and often is life-changing.

Forgiveness

Looking back and not being in the middle of the abuse, it is easier for me to forgive than those still in the midst of abusive, toxic relationships. With my brother and father deceased, my mother with Alzheimer's, and me being much older and wiser, time has taken care of some of the wounds and therapy, and God has taken care of the rest. I believe all that was left was the need to forgive myself, which I have now done. Often the forgiveness starts with us and once that occurs, forgiveness for others comes more easily. It's important in my life not to harbor anger and resentments; it is important for me to feel love and to ask God to take care of the rest.

Being in a strong and positive place in my life is very rewarding but would never have been possible had I not addressed the toxicity head on and resolved the emotions attached to my past. I am always grateful to God for the many bridges of people he placed in my life as therapists, colleagues, supervisors, and friends for this to be possible. Perfection was never something I desired, it was a role I was destined to play. Once I gave up ideas and attachments to perfection, I found true grace. The lies and self-limiting beliefs slowly drifted away, just as the tides in the ocean carry the ships out to the sea, and my life began.

What I learned

My clients come to me with much toxicity from dysfunctional families and upbringings with long-term issues of control, competition, jealousy, rage, abuse, and neglect. Often there is triangulation with individuals by pitting against each other in the family system, and there is always a lack of open communication and a lack of individuals getting their needs met.

Many times individuals do not remember parts of their childhood, and others remember situations they wish to forget. In cases of traumatic events and memories, intensive therapies work best for many. Revisiting the past and restructuring one's core beliefs by working through the emotions is often productive and lasting. Many therapists will say that one does not need to revisit the past and I disagree with that on some levels. For some, the pain of the past is too great and will cause further harm, so it's important to identify the core issues and the goals about revisiting the past. The decision for some of my clients has depended on whether they were seeking a Band-Aid or a complete change and how deep the wounds were that impacted their lives. Often Band-Aids are not big enough to cover the open wounds of the past, but Band-Aids do aid in healing. Everyone is different.

Forgiveness is controversial with many individuals who have been in toxic relationships and/or endured abuse. When individuals forgive, they no longer carry the anger and resentment that previously permeated their being. For some, forgiveness is the right choice, but for others, forgiveness is not the right choice at the time and maybe never. I have no judgments about those who choose not to forgive, each person has to decide what is right.

For some, the best choice is to get out of the situation as quickly as possible and to find safety. When one takes a stand and says no to further dysfunction and abuse, a strong statement is made to let the individuals involved know that abuse is not okay and will no longer be tolerated. Since control is taken and power is given, it's about finding one's power and letting go of the things that have been allowed to control one's life.

Chapter Eleven
Be There for Another

My parents taught us through their example to always be available to those who were broken and to serve others, which has had a tremendous impact on my career choice and my life. I have a tendency to be available to those who are broken emotionally, but my father, in one particular situation, was available to me at a time when I needed him, physically and emotionally.

My needs

One of my earliest memories is of a time when I was around five or six years old. My father had gotten a swing set and put it together for my siblings and me. I remember being filled with excitement! When I saw the beautiful, shiny silver-and-red swing set, I could hardly feel myself breathe. It was magical. It came with two swings, a seesaw, a six-foot slide, and sidebars. The first day we played from sunup to sundown. I decided it was surely heaven on earth. Being a part of a family with little money and very few distractions in our lives outside of working on the farm, this swing set was something that brought me joy beyond my wildest dreams.

My father was mostly a quiet man except for when he would lose his temper; once that happened, he was at no loss for words. He gave one clear directive regarding the swing set. We were to play on the swing set only when supervised. Of course, everyone listened except for me. I did not listen, even then. There was always something a little different about me. Being somewhat free-spirited, I was known for being strong-willed or maybe even a little obstinate at times. You could say I was quite the gutsy child in the family, but not listening to my father with his temper was pretty ridiculous to say the least—the man had hands of steel! His hands were so hard and calloused that they didn't even feel like human hands; they were more like wet leather gloves that had been worn out in the rain and hardened over time. I knew all too well about his hands because I had gotten spanked several times for being a little different and not following his directives. You could say my father didn't know what to do with me, and I really don't think he ever figured it out.

Unfortunately, on the third day after my father had put together this swing set, I decided to play on it all by myself—unsupervised. I'm not sure how long I played, but it seemed like only moments. On the swing set, time would stand still and hours would pass like minutes. Then, suddenly, in a split second, I lost my grip and fell from the side bar. I hit the hard ground with my arm underneath, causing a serious fracture. My ability to think about consequences at that time was gone. In excruciating pain, loud, blood-curling screams began coming out of my mouth, and they must have gotten my father's attention. Out of nowhere, I saw him jet towards me as if his feet were not touching the ground; he rapidly swept me up, cradling me in his large, strong arms for safety. My memory fails me as to what happened after that moment. I just remember that my father had rescued me, and with his loving arms, I was safe, protected, and loved. In that very moment, my father gave me a gift that would be with me forever. This time he was there for me in my brokenness.

My father's needs

However, the first time my father suffered from physical brokenness we realized that he had needs too. He was a very large man, over 6'2" and very stout, as we say in the rural area. He was very proud of his strength and used to arm wrestle with relatives when they visited. He used to throw two one-hundred-pound feedbags over his shoulders and carry them long distances to feed the livestock. For many years, he worked in logging and carpentry or other manual labor jobs. He usually had two or three jobs at any given time. Later, he went to work for companies to get more consistency with paychecks and benefits so as not to worry about paying the bills or having health insurance for the family. For several years, he worked for a utility company, assisting them in building a power station. He changed jobs and finally ended up working for the county government delivering concrete rocks to surface roads around the county in which we lived.

He had a tremendous work ethic of honesty, being on time, and not missing a day, even when he was very sick. Mondays were especially hard for him. In the mornings, he drank one cup of coffee, and it was so strong it was the consistency of syrup; Starbucks didn't exist then, but if so, they would have nothing on my mother's strong coffee. She would put it on the top of the stove, and it would percolate for a long time until it was ready; somehow, she always knew when it was.

Anyways, during the time I was a teenager, my father got up one Monday morning to go to work, had his cup of coffee, which he could hardly hold onto from his shaking due to his withdrawal from alcohol and went off to work. Sometime around noon, my mother got a call that he was at the doctor's office; he had driven his truck to the city gravel dump, and as he was turning the truck bed to dump the gravel out, the truck flipped over. The impact was so great that it had broken his back. Later, I was told that he got out of the gravel truck, walked over to his boss, and told him he was in pain and had to go to the doctor. He even drove himself to the doctor's office in excruciating pain. There was no one there for him that day. We tried to be there for him as much as he would allow.

My dad never believed in inconveniencing others, so it never crossed his mind to do what he needed to do to take care of himself in this situation or in any other; he really didn't know how, and being his own worst enemy, he didn't trust anyone else to help him. Finally, after several months of continuing to try to work, and after much encouragement, he applied for Social Security disability, and when he was denied the disability, he reluctantly found an attorney to help him refile. He had to testify in court, and the whole situation was taking its toll on him. He stayed at home a lot and worried all the time about lack of money and how he was going to make ends meet. Being illiterate and relying on his physical strength his entire life, his self-esteem was at an all-time low, and he continued to drink alcohol and obsess about the future. He went to the mailbox every day to check the mail, hoping to get the approval for disability, but it never came; ironically, it came in the mail a couple of days after his death. There seemed to be no refuge for his pain late in life and no way to heal the brokenness after death.

Others' needs

Cancer has also had an impact on my family with the diagnosis of breast cancer with my mother, one of my sisters, and one of my nieces. They are some of my biggest heroes, and they have carried torches to help many with this diagnosis. Mom and Joyce have been there for others through their pain, and my niece, Cheryl, even developed her own business after her bout with breast cancer. Cheryl works for a retreat center in North Carolina providing a way to be available, through healthy nutrition and love, for those who need someone to be there in their brokenness in dealing with cancer. Oddly, Cheryl lost her job when she had taken time off for surgery after her cancer diagnosis. Being very forgiving, she has come out of her situation much stronger. When she comes back home after a weekend of helping those of her calling, I can easily see the healing that is taking place in her own life, the healing that best occurs from serving others in their brokenness.

What I have learned

The way I help many through their brokenness is by being available and having empathy. There are many sessions I have given for free over the years for those who are unable to pay but still have the desire for healing. Many individuals coming to see me for therapy have various physical diagnoses and issues. Some have been diagnosed with cancer, heart disease, autoimmune diseases, and many other diseases. At times, I am called upon to be an emotional bridge for one who has been broken physically by a car accident, natural disaster, or perhaps a surgery in which things did not go well and the person needs to share his/her deepest fears. Treatment for trauma is a mixed blessing in that I travel with them through the past and present pains of their lowest lows and help them to define their new highs on the other side of their brokenness. I lean on my education, knowledge, training, and the light I have found from dealing with my own past and give of myself through prayer, love, and a gentle touch; when they find their own strength and light, many move on to another level of healing and finding light, which continues through helping others who are broken.

Chapter Twelve
Be Aware of Sensory Connections

Making many bad choices as far back as I can remember was at the top of the list of unresolved issues in the way of my desire to forgive myself. Setting the stage for several of my choices takes me back many years in time. It was Christmastime 1981; it seems like yesterday as I remember it, but most of the time it seems like a thousand years ago. I had been dating someone on and off for around eight years—mostly off; he was in the Army and had spent three years in Germany and over a year in Korea. There were a couple years that I had little contact with him. He was the first real date I ever had when I was fifteen or sixteen.

First date

I had had a date when I was around twelve years old, if you could call it that. It was a triple date with my brother Dan, his date, my sister Joyce, and two of Dan's Army friends. Even though, I don't exactly remember my brother's age, my sister was fourteen and I was twelve. Dan and Joyce squeezed in the back seat with their dates, and I was in the front seat. It was supposed to have been a fun group event at a drive-in movie but ended up in disaster for me; after that night, I had vowed to myself to never date again. The young man I was with was Hispanic and short, and I was attracted to him in a strange sort of way (I had only been around Caucasians mostly, and I was several inches taller than him); he was one of the soldiers Dan had brought home with him for the weekend—he was always bringing guys home with him. It could have been because they had the cars so that he could get a ride home, since we were so poor, or it could have been just because he had lots of friends and felt sorry for them due to being so far from home. I'm sure he could relate to that since he was drafted and never wanted to leave home in the first place. I think they were his family when he was away from home. It wasn't until the year before my brother's passing from this life that he told me his survival in the military was due to being close to his Hispanic friends; he said, "We really took care of each other." It was an interesting comment totally unrelated to the conversation we were having and coming out of the blue from my brother, but I finally got it. He was justifying and even apologizing to me for that one significant night, but it took me a while to connect the dots of his apology. The way the men in my life justify and apologize for things always surprises me; it's like a guessing game of trying to figure out what they mean when they make statements out of the blue. Anyway, by the time Dan brought this up, my thoughts about that night were long gone from my memory and my conscious mind. We so often try to forget the difficult times of the past that cause us pain; for me, I believe it is so that I can move forward. I had not realized that I had blocked out some of the memories completely. Even though I had forgotten, my brother had not.

This particular man, on my first dating experience when I was twelve years old, tried kissing me; our noses smashed up against each other's (like in funny movies), which really hurt, but neither of us knew how to get our noses out of the way. In looking back, I imagine I was his first kiss as well. Seconds afterwards, even though he spoke poor

Be Aware of Sensory Connections

English, he had no trouble with the words, "May I feel?" Not giving me any time to respond, he quickly made an advance. Well, being as unprepared as I was, I reacted quickly! I yelled at him, slapped his hand, moved over to the other side of the car, and demanded that I be taken home. Of course, we were in *his* car, which made things worse, and he and no one else cared enough to listen to me, even then they wanted me to calm down and keep watching and laughing at the movie. Dan and Joyce, in the back seat with their dates, apologized, but no one was willing to leave the movie. They kept saying since we are here "Let's just enjoy the movie" and "We already paid." Easy for them to say! I was violated! I was angry! I was crying! I just wanted to go home to my mother, but no one heard me. Silently, I wept. Being so young and unprepared, I did not know what to do to get out of that situation. No matter what I did or said, it did not matter and it was not enough. Looking back, anything would have been better than sitting there in that car for the next hour or so, which was like an eternity for me. I felt helpless—an all too familiar feeling. With the lack of action of my siblings, I must have decided on a deep level that it was my fault, and that was confirmed by being told to let it go.

Years later, at fifteen or sixteen, I met a man at the steakhouse where I was a waitress. I'll refer to him as X. He was Asian, short, and spoke broken English. X pursued me relentlessly. He ate at the steakhouse often, and everyone there knew him. He was famous in our little town; X was the only Asian-born person that I knew of and was popular and well liked. He was different, which appealed to me in a strange sort of way. He valued education and worked hard. He went to college and worked full-time. X had a great sense of humor and would say things that no one else would consider saying, and mostly, he was determined for me to go out on a date with him. It was hard for me to understand why this person would not take no for an answer. Every time he came into the steakhouse, my heart rate would go up significantly, and I couldn't slow it down. Later, one of my friends told me that was the "flight or fight" response, but I certainly did not know what it was. Then, one day, he called me at work at the beginning of my shift and said he was going to ask me out for the last time and then he would never ask me out again; for whatever reason, I accepted his offer to go on a date. Perhaps it was the ultimatum or maybe that he had tapped into my abandonment issues or it could have been that I just wanted to go out with him to see if he was for real.

It was 1973, and he wanted to go to a movie and out to eat; not knowing the name of the movie, X said he had just gotten us tickets. Well, being from a life of isolation and poverty, I had gone to very few movies; I had gone to school and just worked all the time. I had heard a little about *The Exorcist*, but I would never see anything like that and was not interested in horror movies, especially about a little girl being possessed by demons. At the movie window, I realized the tickets he was purchasing and asked to see something else, but he refused. Once we got into the movie, I asked to leave, but he still refused. He said I didn't have to watch it, that I could just close my eyes. Even in my irritation and anger, I stayed in the movie. I felt unprepared, helpless, and unheard. Familiar? You bet!

I'm not sure why after *The Exorcist* movie incident I continued to go out with him. Perhaps it was because he pursued me relentlessly or because he reinforced the negative feelings I had about myself through the negative things he said about my family and me, but he was also entertaining and fun. Even though he was not what I wanted in a boyfriend, I looked forward to dating him.

Then one night after we had gone out on a date, X wanted to park the car and kiss. I didn't say no to the kissing, but this time he wanted to go further. When I said no, he was furious. He began yelling and started threating to never see me again if I didn't comply and accusing me of lying about caring for him. It went on and on and on. I thought he would never stop. I began to cry, which didn't even phase him, and finally, I gave in; he kept discounting that it was a big deal with it being just from the waist up, and of course, he stated he couldn't understand why I had made it a big deal. I was overwhelmed with tremendous shame and guilt, feeling helpless and unheard—familiar but still devastating. That night I had on my favorite burgundy pantsuit with a lovely yellow blouse that I had purchased on lay-a-way for weeks before I could fully pay for it. After all these years, I still remember what I was wearing and how much I loved that outfit; after that night, I no longer cared about wearing that pantsuit. The outfit was disgusting, and so was I. I hated him and I cared about him at the same time. Confused and discounting my feelings and the sensory experiences of feeling sick and stressed, I was caught up in a pattern of behaviors, and worse, I had no idea. It was a dysfunctional pattern of confusing love, pity, and powerlessness in a relationship. It was the same type of relationship I had witnessed in my family for years, and the same type of relationship I said many times I would never have in my adult life.

X pursued me as much to marry him as he did to date him back in 1973, even though I refused many, many times. He knew how to manipulate me, and I am sure it was easy, but I felt trapped. One night he brought his mother and sister into yet another restaurant where I was working and gave me an engagement ring at the table while I was waiting on them. I didn't say no and just took the ring. The games continued, and I felt totally helpless to change them. I felt so sad for X. In many ways, he grew up like my father, with times of near-starvation, poverty, and abuse. I found myself not wanting to hurt him, but not wanting to be in a relationship with him either. During the years from 1973 to 1981, I was in a fog. I overextended myself by going to high school and college and always working two or three jobs at any given time. Not being in touch with my feelings, I was numb. I had been in a couple of other relationships but they never seemed to work out.

First love

However, there was one man that I truly loved sometime during the eight years before Christmas of 1981. He was very special. He was handsome with sweet brown eyes, and when he looked at me, I could feel my knees weaken. He was about my height or a little taller; he didn't drink alcohol, which was a good thing, and I felt his love for me when I was near him. He came from an alcoholic home like me, except his mother had gotten a divorce when he was young, and he was an only child. He told me a story about his father hurting him in front of others at a baseball game as a child and I felt so sad for him to have had such an experience.

For me, I had met the man of my dreams. He was very handsome and popular; he had long hair, and whereas I thought it was attractive, my father certainly did not. When he came to the door to pick me up for our first date, my father lit into him like a rocket from hell. It started with a handshake, and then, out of nowhere, my dad was calling him names and telling him that if he didn't have the money or if he was too damn lazy to get a haircut, he would certainly give him the money and transport him to the barber shop. I was unprepared, upset, embarrassed, and everything else, and the young man just sat there. I believe he feared for his life; he did leave after a while and told me he would call later, but he never said anything back to my father. He did call me later and our relationship continued; he would drive up in the front yard, and I would go out to the car to meet him. I could read my father pretty well by this time, and it was very upsetting to my father that I would openly be so rebellious to him. He must have felt guilty because he never tried to stop me from dating him.

Being so in love, I became completely intimate with this man, emotionally and physically. He was my first. Of course, I already felt damaged because of what happened with X, so, to me, it didn't really matter what I did anymore. Unfortunately, the relationship didn't last; I had the strong sense that he was seeing other girls. I think sometimes either we know things or we just believe they are occurring, but there were just too many signs. I believe my fear of intimacy and non-trust is what ended our relationship. I had never really been intimate with anyone on an emotional or physical level, and I couldn't be then—it was too scary. Plus, to choose him over my father's wishes would never work. I was risking my ability to be loved unconditionally by my dad, which is what I believed I always wanted in my existence anyway. So I had my brother Royce deliver him a letter at school, since they were both attending the same college, and the relationship crumbled afterwards. It was a "Dear John" letter breaking up with him but not really with teasing sentences at the end. Not only did my relationship with this young man that I loved disintegrate, my relationship with Royce changed as well, and I don't believe it ever was as strong afterwards; Royce just told me to never ask him to deliver anything else. This boyfriend and I tried somewhat to mend the relationship later, but it was too hard. There was just too much water under the bridge to move forward. With a broken heart, I moved on.

After our breakup, I participated in a hometown beauty pageant and won. Had it not been for my first love, I never would have had the nerve to enter the pageant. He had gotten engaged to a beauty queen, and when I found out, I thought if I won a beauty pageant he would come back to me, which didn't happen. My dear brother Royce, as forgiving as he was, was there at the pageant as well as my mom, dad, and my dear sisters Gail and Joyce. Royce had written me the sweetest letter, and I have it still today. Others in my family were there for me and they were so proud, but I was still empty inside, even more so. The man I loved was not there.

The years 1975 and 1976 were bittersweet as I shifted from not being noticed to being seen all the time—way more than I ever wanted to be seen. The emptiness inside me expanded as I went through that year. I didn't know enough, I didn't smile right enough, my teeth were not perfect enough, I was never thin enough, my voice was not good enough; the list went on and on and on. The two men who aspired for a winner in the Miss South Carolina pageant transported me anywhere and everywhere to get me the training and experiences I needed to succeed and spent a lot of money taking me to places and out to eat. I felt appreciative of them but indebted to them, and there was no end to the obstacles I faced. How could I compete in a state pageant with everything stacked against me? My mother even borrowed money from the credit union at work to make sure I had the nicest and most expensive clothes, but even with that, it was not enough. Coming from poverty, I could not compete with the other young women who had come from riches—that was just the way it was. I persevered through that year and was determined to enter another pageant later to prove that I was good enough and make a successful life for myself. Two years later, when I was finally able to financially afford it, I got braces on my teeth and still had the dream to do something great in beauty pageants and perhaps in modeling. In 1980, my braces were off, and I had finished all my requirements to graduate from a four-year college. It was to be my time.

A change in direction

Then, when it was Christmastime in 1981, a few situations occurred that changed my life path forever. I was at my parent's house, preparing to celebrate Christmas with them, and X showed up. Everyone else left, and my parents went to bed. They were tired, and my dad had been drinking, of course. X and I had a tumultuous relationship, and I had broken it off several months before. The engagement was short-lived; I decided I never planned to marry him. Looking back, there was always so much drama with X, and I never really felt any peace with him. I felt powerlessness, but it was familiar.

That night he began to ask me over and over and over to marry him and to go to California with him, where he was stationed with the military. I said no multiple times, which was insignificant to him;

Be Aware of Sensory Connections

he knew by that time that my personality was more of a chameleon than anything else. I decided to leave from my parent's house to go back to my apartment, and he followed in his car; it was twenty-five miles to my apartment then, but that night it seemed like hundreds of miles. I remember a couple of times getting the tremendous urge not to go to the apartment and to go far, far away, and even my car revved up when I stopped at the red lights, or maybe I imagined that it did. Perhaps it was God and the angels trying to intervene, but even with my intense feelings of dread, I drove on robotically. My body was screaming at me to listen—I had a headache, stomachache, and felt sick as I drove. He was behind me in his car that night, and when we arrived at the apartment, he continued to ask me over and over again to marry him and said I would never see him again if I did not. It was always ultimatums with him; I did as he asked or it was nothing. With my insecurities and my abandonment issues, he knew how to manipulate me. He would not be quiet or let me rest until I acquiesced. The next morning, we went to a minister's house, and he performed a marriage ceremony, but since there was nothing signed, we weren't officially married (even I knew that). Thankfully, there was a way out of this disaster I had gotten myself into, or so I thought. After leaving the minister's house, I bailed; I don't even remember where I went, but I went somewhere to clear my head all day. This was insanity! How could I have done this? I was gone and didn't call anyone or let anyone know how to contact me for at least twelve hours. At that time, cell phones didn't exist the way they do today, so no one knew where I was, not even my mom with whom I usually stayed in close contact.

Later, I went back to my apartment and X was there, waiting for me in his car. I let him in, and after arguing, which was typical, I let him stay the night. The next morning, very early, I heard knocking at the door—*Oh my God!* It was my parents. My *father* was at my apartment door, and worse, I was in bed with a man to whom I was not married.

Oh my God! The shame and embarrassment were tremendous! How could I face my dad? What could I do? I wanted to run; I wanted to hide. Oh my God! The knocking got louder, and I quickly got my housecoat on and went downstairs. When I let them in, I saw the sadness and the worry in their faces, but I sensed the relief that they could see me. It was the look parents have when their children are in life-threatening situations, like car accidents or natural disasters, but they live through it. I had seen those looks before, but never with me. I had always been the "good child" and tried not to cause trouble.

It was then that they told me X had called them multiple times the day before, and they were worried sick. X had told them everything. He had been berating them the same way he did me. He had told them multiple times that we were married under God. In the moment I thought, *Oh my God, what was I to do?* They said that when they told X on the phone that they didn't know where I was, he accused them of lying to him. *What a mess I had created. Oh my God!*

My parents left my apartment that morning, and I realized that I was in serious trouble. The worst part was that I could never, ever face my father again. That day was not a good day for me, to say the least. We had another Christmas gathering at my parent's house, and I showed up briefly to tell them that I was in fact getting married to X. The next morning at the same preacher's house, I married X, and this time, I did sign the marriage license. With the sick feeling in my stomach and with a broken heart for my losses, I knew I had made a huge mistake, but I was in too deep. My family and my reputation with them were more important to me than my dreams.

The marriage continued for sixteen years, and we had three children. I did not grow up believing in divorce, and X made it clear he did not either. A multitude of issues occurred throughout our marriage. I continued to give my power away to X but started resenting the person I was and certainly blamed him for the majority our problems. After therapy and receiving my master's degree, I was able to finally end the marriage. What I realized was that it was over when I could be indifferent to him. When I was caught up in the drama of love and hate, I was still attached somehow to him. Finding indifference was more in line with being able to leave the dysfunction. After finding peace with myself, I was open to new and different relationships, so I recognized the unhealthy patterns that got me into the marriage that I stayed in for sixteen years.

Today, there is a man at the gym where I go for exercise that seeks me out when I am there. He is short, speaks with a heavy British accent, and is of a different race. Of course, I am attracted to him in a strange sort of way. He has asked me out twice already, and I have refused, but he always tries to engage me in conversation. As I feel the awareness of my body and feel the sick feelings in my stomach and the tightness in my chest, I nod and say hello as I walk in an opposite direction of wherever he is headed. I chuckle silently as I say to myself, "The next man in my life is going to be of my choosing." Being aware of the sensory connections to the patterns of my life, I have found the light into an amazing self-awareness.

What I have learned

Once clients have made the decision that things are to change, it's important for them to take a good look at what got them to where they are. Then they can start doing things differently to get different results. Often they are unaware of their senses and how their bodies are reacting to situations. When the numbness subsides, they begin developing awareness into how they can use their own internal barometers to make better decisions.

The many issues that concern us today are the most deeply rooted issues that create the most internal conflicts. Many times, I have seen clients for numerous visits before they address what is really the root cause of why they come to therapy in the first place. Many don't even know what the root issues are until they pull back the layers of shame, guilt, anger, and unresolved feelings. Once the secrets are spoken, they are able to move forward more freely. Judgment is released, and forgiveness and peace fill the void. Goals can be obtained once the clouds of confusion are removed.

There are many situations that leave their footprints on us, and certainly, they are not always positive. Many of them are sensory, and all of us are triggered and continue repetitive patterns in life, often without the realization of such. So many times the responsibility of traumatic events is displaced onto oneself, even though it was not something that could have been prevented or perhaps it was something so age-inappropriate that there was true helplessness and powerlessness. Often, it is the children that are unprotected; others (caregivers, family, and friends) may react in a particular way, creating doubt, and the child develops a belief that whatever happened is his/her fault. Knowing that this is a self-limiting and erroneous belief is important in finding light.

Sexual abuse is an issue that takes its toll; putting it mildly, it damages self-esteem, confidence, the ability to love and set boundaries, and inhibits true intimacy with others. Putting it more strongly, sexual abuse is a crime against a person's soul. Many I have treated feel they are damaged beyond measure at the core of their being; they believe there is no way to resolve the self-hatred, but when they do resolve it, the time it takes is well worth the effort.

Chapter Thirteen
Learn from Synchronicity

Something happened to me during the time I had fallen from grace that significantly impacted my choices as I moved away from a dark time. Not too long before this darkness, I had resigned from a high-level position with a behavioral health company where I had been employed for sixteen years. I had worked hard and moved up the ranks over time; the people there had become like family to me. I thought I could make it financially without a full-time job (I had two part-time jobs that I decided to keep), but I soon discovered that giving up two-thirds of my monthly salary and all my benefits was not the smartest move I could have made. Looking back, I believe I was just burned out more than anything at the time I resigned, but I had a mortgage, car payments, credit card payments, etc. Embarrassingly, I decided to call up some of my colleagues and find out if there were job openings at other agencies. Fortunately, I was able to contact an acquaintance who offered me a position; the position was a lower level position than what I had held previously, but I would supposedly do less work and supervise fewer employees. Also, she was retiring, so her position would be a possibility. I should have remembered that "If it sounds too good to be true, it is." Well, I soon found that I was miserable. Anything and everything that could have gone wrong did with this job; that's the best way I know to explain it. It was evident to me that I was in the wrong place at the wrong time. The promotion did not come through for me; the company hired a man from another state, and he became my supervisor. They brought him in paying him way more money than me, and one of the first things he did was buy a huge, expensive vehicle. To think of it, everything about him was expansive: his muscles, his vehicle, his expectations, his presence, etc.

There was this one particular time I had been told that I should attend a statewide meeting the following day and represent the agency. My first thought was that I could call in sick, but I was afraid I would get in trouble somehow if I did that. I thought maybe I should come up with another excuse, but I was afraid that anything I came up with would cause negative results. I cringed at the thought of attending this meeting but saw no way out of it, and the shame I felt was overwhelming. It was clear to me that I had made some bad decisions (especially the decision about taking this job), but I did not want everyone attending this meeting from all over the state to know about them. I wanted to keep them hidden, and more, I wanted to be hidden. That day and night seemed to go on *forever*! I went to bed at ten that night, only to lie in bed to perseverate and ruminate about how horrible the next day was going to be. After hours went by, I knew I had to sleep at least a couple of hours to function the next day; after all, I did have to drive several hours to that ridiculous meeting. I decided to pray, and pray I did! I prayed for help to get out of having to face all the people at this meeting. I prayed earnestly not to be in the upcoming embarrassing situation and asked that "this cup pass from me." I prayed and prayed and prayed and finally fell asleep. Then the alarm clock went off, and it was time to face the day. Having no idea how I would make it through the day, I quickly got dressed and traveled to work. Upon arrival, I realized that my prayers had not been answered; I remember saying something silently to God

Learn from Synchronicity

to the effect of "Gee, thanks, God," and my thoughts were that once again my prayers were not answered.

Sometime around ten that morning, I received a call that would have a tremendous impact on my day and my life. Interestingly, I do not even remember who was on the other end of the phone, I just remember the words, "…she died last night. . . she just appeared to stop breathing sometime in the night…no one knows what happened…she was at home alone with the two children…the children were still asleep when her mother found her early this morning." Silence overcame me, and then overwhelming thoughts came and grief consumed me. She was my niece by marriage. This beautiful, young mother, caring nurse, and many other things was gone. How could this be? I thought to myself, I had prayed for years for her to have a child. She and her husband wanted children more than anything. To leave her young children motherless, how could this be?

Saying my goodbyes at work, I stumbled out of the office and went down the elevator the five, dreadful floors to the parking lot. I remember catching a glimpse of my supervisor in his huge vehicle as I walked out, but it did not matter, and he did not matter anymore. I didn't even acknowledge him. For me, he had shrunk in size significantly to a very tiny form, unrecognizable just in the last few minutes. I remember tripping over my feet a couple of times as I walked to my car and do not remember the drive to my house. The dread of my thoughts had synchronized with the time that she died and it was over the top. At the same time I was praying to God to get out of going to a ridiculous meeting, she left her two beautiful young children and husband. I questioned God, I questioned myself, I questioned justice, and I just questioned and questioned why such a horrible thing would happen.

The next few days were a fog for me with so many mixed emotions. I felt so sad about the loss and wondered how all who loved her would get through this time. I drove two hours to the events prior to the funeral and back again to attend the funeral. I never spoke to anyone about the synchronicity of the events of that night; they just never made sense to me. There was no rational way that I could have, in any way, been responsible, but why did it happen the way that it did and why did I feel so horrible? This precious young woman had not even crossed my mind the several days before her death. It made no sense; I asked God why was this synchronized?

Finally, I found peace with this loss in searching for truth and being determined to become a better, stronger person. I was able to work through the pain of the loss in a safe environment at a weekend therapy training at the Wellness Institute, which was a huge blessing. One of my basic beliefs for many years has been that there are no coincidences and that all things that are synchronized are meant to happen.

Afterwards, what I integrated into my life is to give God respect and save the "let this cup pass from me" only for when I am being literally crucified as Jesus was, which has not happened, or if it is truly a life or death matter. It sounds so ridiculous to me now that I prayed that prayer about something I could have easily changed and that I didn't trust God to have his will to be done in my life. Also, I integrated into my life to make decisions that I know are in my best interest and in my highest good with confidence before going to God to bail me out. If something does not feel right to me or is bothering me, I let the people know that need to know, including supervisors—especially supervisors. Then I have faith that God will take care of the rest or will guide me to whatever decisions are best for me and those around me. Sometimes things that we feel we cannot discuss are just too big for us, and we should process them in a safe environment and give them to God as we know and feel God. It is up to us to pay attention to the synchronicity in our lives so that we may choose peace with ourselves and with God and attract the positives; also, it is important for me not to feel responsible for the negative occurrences in the lives of others. It is a boundary that serves me well as I move forward in the light.

What I have learned

Often, I find that clients have guilt around issues that have absolutely nothing to do with them, much like my niece's death. In some of their views, they have been blamed for so many occurrences that they believe anything and everything that goes wrong is somehow their fault. In working with my clients and in my own life experiences, I have found that often when we think positive and give positive thoughts out into the world, they come back to us; I have also found that when we dwell on negativity, it comes back to us as well. Many things happen in lives that are unexplainable, but it doesn't mean that individuals are to blame. It is kind of like situations are coincidental but they are just too strange to be coincidental.

Chapter Fourteen
Assert Clear Boundaries

My parents did not have good boundaries and had no real way to teach something they did not know. Also, I was with them very little due to their time constraint of taking care of the others in the family and working all the time. My boundaries were violated numerous times. I am sure they didn't realize that boundary violations were not healthy for us. My parents never had a second thought about telling me or my siblings to hug relatives even though we didn't feel comfortable doing so. Another way in which they had poor boundaries was their inability to say no and set limits with others. Even getting off the phone with someone when they needed to hang up was difficult for them—they never wanted to hurt someone's feelings. For me, it was important to figure out what my personal boundaries were because they are different for everyone. It was also important for me to give a voice to my boundaries; others are raised differently, and they may not know what our boundaries are unless we are clear and let them know.

The first way in which I developed boundaries was in learning how to set limits and how to say no. I found that since most everyone has his/her own agenda, it was important for me to decide how to set limits that wouldn't create drama or ill will with those I love dearly.

One of the limits I set in my family of origin was to live two hours away. Another way in which I set boundaries is to plan and have firm decisions about what I am going to do. My boundaries are guided further by paying attention to messages from my body about when things are okay or not. I feel nausea or tightness in parts of my body when things are not right for me, and I address the issues.

Boundaries with others

Taking a job working for the state in downtown Atlanta several months ago has been an interesting experience. Having twenty-one years towards state retirement, it was time to go back and fulfill the rest of the twenty-five to thirty years to retire since that's the American way—to have enough money to retire and travel and spend more time with family. It's the goal that most of us work towards and would be nice.

Well, one of my early lessons was that not everyone gets the best parking. I quickly found out that there was not enough parking close to the state offices; parking was offered to me at a discount of $20 a month, but it was a half mile away. Quickly, I took it since staying active is important to me, and I decided it would be a nice advantage to have at least a one-mile walk daily. The parking deck is located at Georgia State University, so I decided it could not be that bad. After all, all three of my children had been students at Georgia State at various times, so I decided it must be safe enough. I had heard stories from time to time about the street people and the homeless, and I thought I would be prepared—little did I know.

In February, it was cold in Atlanta for me but even colder for the homeless. Every time I passed by those that were huddled in corners or asleep under multiple blankets and quilts at the sides of buildings, I would feel so sorry for them. I had a home to go to and a warm bed, and they did not. Often, I would wonder why I was so privileged to have a warm house and a warm bed and they were not. There were a few times in the beginning that I let some of them know how sad I felt for them. It did not take me long to realize that if I engage in a conversation with them or even give them eye contact, I would often be followed or harassed for money for at least a block or more. Even though sometimes I wanted to, I didn't give them money. Most of them have been very polite and start with, "Excuse me, ma'am" or "Do you have some change to spare?" but I have had a couple of occasions when they have become fairly aggressive with what they say and how they act. I figured out that I have less difficulty when I ignore them and give them little eye contact. It is hard for me but in my best interest. The firm boundary of letting them know that I have limits has stopped the majority of the individuals from approaching me on the streets; also, it has stopped them from following me or waiting for me the next day. I can still help them and sometimes leave food for them. I can help them in other ways too that do not have to be shared. My mother always said that the Bible says, "One should give in secret for blessings from God."

It's important that we are aware of how we respond to others, and it is important for us to be aware of our environments and make good choices.

What I have learned

Many of my clients have specific issues with boundaries and fall prey to predators over and over again. They come to me feeling damaged and wounded and are not clear on how to change. Many of them have said to me that they must have something on their foreheads that is a marking for others saying, "Come and abuse me." They are very strong and insightful individuals who sincerely want to change how they live their lives but do not know how to change whatever "this" is. They have lost their ability to judge and discern when a person and/or an environment is unsafe, and they are unsure of their boundaries. Helping them to develop confidence in paying attention to their bodies and subtleties within their environments lead them to a better ability and understanding to make decisions that are in their best interest. The best way to do this is to go back to the beginning of when they lost their abilities to be able to trust themselves and trust their bodies' signals. Often they will say that it doesn't make sense, and my response is that it doesn't have to. It just needs to give you guidance on what you want to change and how to change it.

It's important to know that in situations where individuals were victimized through acts of crime, violence, and abuse that I do not feel they bring these actions on themselves or in any way deserve them; I do not believe we should be tolerant. Sometimes justice does not happen in our lifetime; I am thankful that there are laws to protect people, and I am thankful for the military, the justice system, and law enforcement for all they do to protect. Also, I am grateful that laws can be changed to provide more protection and that we can be change agents and provide advocacy for ourselves and others.

Chapter Fifteen
Find Creativity

For many years, I gave up my desire to sing. Perhaps, it was due to hardship or the lack of recognition that I deserved to feel and to send love through my singing to others, but there is probably nothing I like better than singing. I love to sing and I love music. Anything from Christian hymns, songs of the '70s and the '80s, and a variety of other music feeds my soul. In my childhood, I sang in the choir at church, and in my high school years and afterwards, I sang solos in church and branched out to sing in weddings and at other events. As with most things, the more I did it, the better I became and the more comfortable I became getting up in front of large crowds. My love of singing and music started early with my family. My dad had a love for country music and always watched Porter Wagner and Dolly Parton on television. I do believe that was his favorite TV program. He played country music more when he was drinking alcohol on the weekends than any other time, and it was the depressing songs about sadness and heartache, so there are specific country singers that are not particularly to my liking. My mother on the other hand would sing, but she could not carry a tune. She would sing lullabies to me, and the songs she sang were like the melodious sounds of saints. I loved how she would sing to me as I fell asleep at night; she sang from her heart and it was some of the sweetest sounds ever heard.

My brothers and sisters loved to sing and had favorite songs they would sing as they worked in the garden or did their chores. My father would load us up in the back of his pickup truck and take us to the country store to hear banjo-picking and singing on Saturday nights, and those were some of the good times. I still love some country music, and I think "Rocky Top" is my all-time favorite country song, even though Tennessee was never my home. In my high school and some of my college years, I worked at Oconee State Park at the concession stand in the summers and got involved in the square dancing they had on Saturday nights. I looked forward to those Saturday nights.

The creative moments with my mother were times in the kitchen. She had tremendous patience, and she would pull up a chair next to her, pick me up, and allow me to stand in it, and she would teach me how to cook and bake. She was the best at cooking, and what made the difference was that she had such joy while she was in the kitchen; it was as if she infused the food with her love. I learned that from her, and anytime there's a special event or if I am stressed, I find my joy as a whip up meals in the kitchen.

My creativity in my love for writing has just come to me the last few years. Since school was not something I enjoyed and writing never came easy for me, I did not take extra writing classes and never, ever thought it would be one of the creative skills that would propel me forward. A dear friend told me years ago when I was in graduate school that I was a good writer, but I did not believe it. I was going through hard times and thought she said that more because she cared about me; interesting how the people who love us see strengths in us far before we see them in ourselves. What I find now is that my writing brings me a depth of peace and joy. When I put on paper what is in my heart, I find happiness and light.

It's up to us to find what makes our hearts sing. It's an interesting process when doors open and discovery happens. From my perspective, it's what I put my heart and soul into that makes the difference in my happiness and in where I find my creativity that brings me closer to the light and closer to others.

What I have learned

Many who have come to me for therapy believe they have lost their ability to be creative. So many times the focus of treatment is on changing their self-limiting beliefs. Once they are able to get beyond their beliefs and feel better about themselves, the creativity comes more easily. When someone feels damaged or flawed, it is difficult to feel that one deserves to feel joy. Many of my clients have histories of singing, dancing, playing musical instruments, painting, cooking, being active in sports, writing, and other forms of creativity that they have given up completely. The very areas that could have a direct impact on their feelings and improve their quality of life have ceased to exist. A significant area of growth is when they find their way back to themselves and embrace their creativity. Once they find what feeds their souls and makes their hearts sing, their energy shifts to moving in a more positive direction.

Chapter Sixteen
Make Self-Care a Top Priority

My parents were both at the point of physical collapse most of the time. They had well-defined roles with my dad and the boys being responsible for the outside with the heavy, hard labor and my mom and the girls being responsible for taking care of the children and the inside of the house. The only exceptions were when there were big projects that took the entire family to complete; these projects were when we had animals to slaughter (I so hated those times) and, at times, when needed to work in the vegetable garden and taking care of the crops at harvest time. When my mother wasn't quoting the Bible, she had other interesting sayings and rhymes she said over and over again and this is one: "A man works from sun to sun and a woman's work is never done." She had this way of letting us know that was the way it was and we couldn't do anything about it.

Self-care was considered selfishness when I grew up, and it was unacceptable. The only time someone put herself first was during illness; otherwise, she was to do what was needed and necessary for the family. My mother would tell us stories of being hospitalized five years prior to my birth for what she called a nervous breakdown, and when I think back, it seems like it must have been depression, exhaustion, and, most likely, postpartum depression. My dad did take his nights off after dark and would sit and smoke cigarettes and drink alcohol some during the week but would drink a lot on weekends, and he would always rest on Sundays, unless there was an emergency. It seems like my mom and dad had both trained themselves not to feel. It was a household of addictions to food, cigarettes, alcohol, work, perfection, and secrets. Not that I blame them, I think they were doing what they knew to do. It was a way of life.

Weight loss

My siblings would always be on diets on and off except for Dan and Joyce who never gained weight; my parents would work on their weight loss from time to time, but most of us struggled to keep our own weight down. Contrary to this, the one area that we wanted and never scrimped on was food. We rarely ever went out to eat, but we always had plenty of food to eat at home. We had good meals and had meat or protein at every meal, along with vegetables and bread. The very best was the sweets, and we always had plenty of desserts. It was important to my father that we always had plenty to eat. He had lived through the great depression and had very little food as a child; he wanted to make sure he and his family always had plenty to eat.

We always had our meals together, which might be a blessing in other families, but for the most part, it wasn't a blessing for us. When my dad said anything at all at mealtime, it was a time when he chose to say negative things, and we were supposed to sit there and take whatever he dished out with his words. Countless verbal arguments began at the supper table, and we were to stuff down our feelings with food. He and my mom had no idea that it was a great training ground for anyone to develop digestive problems, obesity, or other eating disorders.

The powerlessness in my family of origin was pervasive and was bleeding over into all aspects of our lives. Through my experiences, I found that if my life were to change and impact other's lives, I had to be proactive and put myself first. With my father's death from a massive heart attack and my mother's diabetes and Alzheimer's, I knew that for me to continue to be healthy and independent, it was important for me to put myself first—for myself and for my children. It is my wish to have my children be able to communicate with me when I'm eighty years old, and if it is preventable, which sometimes it isn't, I want to do what I need to do to be healthy.

What I learned

In my experience, when I started changing one aspect of my life, other aspects followed with more ease. When I stopped overspending and overusing credit cards and gained control of my spending, I began to stop overeating as much; when I made sleep and rest important, I started exercising; when I began sharing the secrets of my past, the shame and embarrassment dissipated; when I was able to release my anger and fear and the dislike of myself, I found love, acceptance, and forgiveness; when I let go of feeling that I had to control or needed to control others, I found my power. The list goes on and on; it has been a domino effect of positives in my life, and it is available to all of us once we start taking action.

Many I see for treatment put themselves last when it comes to their own needs. Most often, it is attributed to perfectionism, and sometimes it is due to taking care of others and having lots of responsibilities. Unfortunately, many have fibromyalgia, chronic pain, cancer, and a myriad of other physical illnesses that have developed over time by neglecting to have good self-care. Some of them are single with no children; some are single parents that do as much as they possibly can for their children and, when they have any free time, work at home, pick up extra shifts, or take on additional jobs.

Others that are in relationships and have children are sometimes fortunate to have help but others do not. Some are young and some are grandparents. They all have different life challenges and obligations. Many express that they are sleep deprived and have difficulty sleeping due to worry about the next day and the future. I hear many stories about not being good enough, right enough, or anything enough. They speak of never making the mark they set out to make and falling short of the expectations of themselves and others. Some have issues with weight and feel bad about their appearance but some do not. They usually have the commonality of feeling stuck with no real way out of their situations. Some are controlled by guilt, fear, anger, shame, and sadness, and they express powerlessness to do things differently.

One paradox is that clients often come for sessions to feel better in their current situation but not always to change; most often, one wants to be heard, figure out how to change someone else, or how to feel better in the same situation. I so get this because I have been there myself. We can be such mirror images of each other. We see in others what we are challenged within ourselves. Ironically, once individuals are truly heard and process his/her own needs, they figure out that it is up to them to change their situations; when this occurs, one starts to realize what is important and how to gain power to do things differently, which will ultimately have the result of changing their situations and their lives positively. It always starts with one's self. I do get it; you see, it's not just textbook for me. Good self-care is worth the effort.

Chapter Seventeen
Become Grounded

One of my strengths is that I am very open-minded. Before I did the work I needed to do on myself and before I worked in the field of behavioral health, I was much more rigid in my thinking. There's so much that I've seen and experienced that being rigid in my thinking does not come into play as much anymore. Over the past few years, I've developed a curiosity and interest in alternative therapies and have seen many find improvements through them. I have also enjoyed studying some astrology. Since I am not an expert in the field of astrology, I will leave the definition and teachings to astrologists. However, in finding out that in my natal chart (a chart astrologists use) I have the presence of five fire signs, along with my water sign from being born under the sign of Cancer, it was helpful to me. I found it to be a way of opening my mind as to how I view situations and a way to be less hard on myself when I take action. Another way in which it is helpful is in understanding some of areas of importance in taking care of myself. Since the rest of my planets were in water signs at my birth, it's very important for me to live a life where I put some effort into bringing in earth energy to be more balanced. A few ways of doing this are in spending time out in nature, being active, meditating, and being around those with more earth energy, such as those born in months of earth signs. These can be considered anchors to assist in balance and in being grounded. Being grounded from my perspective is a way of feeling solid and having the absence of confusion or anxiety. When one is grounded, he/she is present and able to see, feel, and think clearly. It creates a balance of being able to move forward with flexibility, confidence, and ease.

My mother and father were open-minded in some areas and always bought almanacs; they lived by them to plant their crops and paid a lot of attention to the variations in the moon and the impact of a full moon when it was in the sky. My mother had an ability to tell time by looking at where the sun was at any time during the day. Both of my parents told us of the Cherokee Indian heritage in our lineage, and even though I do not know how much and who they were, I am sure of it. Being poor and uneducated, my family never kept records of the past, and it was all word of mouth. My best recollection is that it was in the lineage of a great-grandmother on both of my parents' sides of the family, which makes sense to me. My father loved the Cherokee Indians and took us to the Blue Ridge Mountains at times to speak to them and hear their music when I was very young, and it was quite significant; I still remember the experience and how much my father felt at ease with them. Growing up with such rich Native American cultural experiences helps me understand my love of cultures and the various ways in which people view the world and live their lives. Nature and living from the land is a good way to stay grounded, and I find myself wanting to spend more time in nature when I need to feel grounded.

Some of the ones that help me to be grounded in times of great pain were the people in my life that were there for me when I needed them. Since I had such difficulty trusting in my childhood, it has always been important for me to choose friends that I could trust; I have truly been blessed beyond measure. We don't always think about our needs and how they will be addressed, but my friends have all been there for me when I needed them; my friends encouraged me to push beyond barriers and be successful, and they have been with me every step of the way on my journey. Many blessings come from many different directions and angles. My friends' and colleagues' love, teachings, loyalty through the hard times, and being bridges in my healing have given me many memories of how to be grounded in difficult times.

What I learned

Hard times always resurface but in different ways. We all go through times of loss and pain and hardship and times of need; it is the memories of how we survived before that helps us to get to the other side. Whatever reminds us of how we got past the difficulty before will help us to be grounded in the hard times and propel us forward to the positive times in finding light ahead.

Over time, clients that are from different cultures, backgrounds, upbringings, and ethnicities have come to me for help. Often, they need something or someone to anchor them or bring them back to a feeling of safety and calmness. Many times, this feeling of being grounded comes from items that are symbolic or individuals that impacted their lives in a positive direction. Being grounded can stem from memories of how people were there for them in various hard times and times of need. Usually they are priceless and timeless and are primarily or singularly important to that one individual, but they are so significant and instrumental that a memory or item can help in finding tranquility in times of chaos and pain. Special rings, stones, charms, and rocks are some of the items. Handwritten letters, pictures, and memories of individuals can all be significant in helping one to find solidness in critical times of need.

Chapter Eighteen
Take Action

In all my many changes throughout my life, I have never had that magical moment where I knew beyond a shadow of doubt that I was making the right decision. Even in my divorce, I never got to the place of confidence before I made the change that it was the definite and right thing to do. However, in my divorce, I gained powerful experience and insight on how to change. It is defined more by me as movement forward to the point of no return. I rehearsed in my mind over and over what I was going to do and made small steps, very small steps forward until I met my goal.

For other changes, I first decided in my mind what I was going to do. I read books and did research on what others had done to be successful, and I talked to friends, other social workers, and therapists about how lasting change comes about with individuals. I figured out for me to make changes that were difficult, I had to have consequences in place that would make it hard for me not to make the changes. Unfortunately, I failed miserably with one of the first changes; I enlisted my children for help and here's what I did: I talked to each of my three children and told them I would give them each five hundred dollars if I didn't lose a certain amount of weight in a certain amount of time. Of course, my children were thrilled when I didn't lose the weight—looking back I think that it was my own self-sabotage at its best! They had never seen that kind of money, and getting five hundred dollars was extra special for them. On a very positive note, I learned a very rich lesson, or rather a poor one, depending on how you wish to look at it.

My next change did happen. I had worked at a company for over sixteen years and had worked hard to move up in the ranks; I was responsible for several departments and we did good work. Not only did we do good work, we were known for the good work. I remember one day being called into my supervisor's office and told that my job was changing. Not only was my job changing, she had already decided with others in the company how it was going to change without getting any of my input, and more, I was the chosen one to make it happen. I was unhappily surprised to say the least. I had worked for this woman for a few years and felt that I had been loyal and honest with her. To me, the betrayal was significant; you see, my jobs in mental health have never been "just business" to me. Prior to this, I had been working many long hours and had even taken on an extra project to work with a group of individuals affected by a natural disaster. Then others had decided what was going to happen to the staff I had hired and the departments for which I was responsible? Really? And I was supposed to not only go along with it, I was supposed to be in charge of it, and make like it was my idea? Really? I thought, *This is behavioral health?* We're in the helping field and we do this to each other? Being loyal and trying to stay with it, I agreed to do as I was told even though every part of my body was screaming that I should not. As the changes began, it was mass pandemonium. People didn't know what to do or how to do it, and the plans for change were seriously flawed. Plus, the staff I had supervised for years were not given choices either. I tried to tell my supervisor that it was not working, but she didn't listen, which was so familiar. After watching the absurdity for a few days, witnessing a young adolescent and his family finally wait two full days to be seen for a mental health evaluation (which could have easily been my family with my sister), and having one of my dedicated, loyal employees take early retirement, I found my power. Even though at the time I didn't love myself enough to find it for myself, I found it through my belief in social justice and caring for others. I decided to resign, but before I did, I booked two nonrefundable tickets to Hawaii for ten days for my daughter and me, and I booked them at the busiest time for this particular company; I knew there was no chance that I would be given time off, and no chance that I would back out. When I resigned, I was at the point of no return; I made the change. There were difficult times afterwards, and my life would have been easier financially had I stayed, but it was a good decision for me. I have learned things about myself through that transition that I never would have learned had I stayed there.

Unfortunately, once I left this company, I found that there are many other work environments where betrayal runs deep, and even though it is all justified in the name of "just business," it doesn't make it right. The greatest lesson I learned from this company and others that followed was that the betrayal that runs deepest is that of self-betrayal. I had betrayed myself by leaving as a victim and not advocating for my rights, and I did that in other positions and other parts of my life as well. Then I made the decision that never, ever again would I allow myself to be victimized by companies, organizations, or individuals, and never will I betray myself. It was a radical shift in thinking, but one we all are able to make when we stand to take action and make a change for ourselves and our higher good. There are many changes I've been able to make since that time, and for me, they have become easier with practice. It begins with the decision to change, rehearsing it in your mind, and then following through by having consequences that make it hard *not* to go through with the change. However, it's important to make transitions slowly and when you can effectively deal with them; no one else can tell you when that time is, you must be open and conscious as to how and when it is best for you.

Weight Loss

Weight loss for me has always been the most difficult challenge. I love to eat, and I love to cook and bake—not a good combination for someone who has a tendency to gain weight easily. Also, one of my favorite hobbies is eating different foods at different restaurants. Whether the food is Indian, Vietnamese, Italian, Korean, Thai, Mexican, American, I like them all and have favorites in every type of restaurant. For me to give up good food is totally out of the question. Another challenge for me is portion sizes; as I have been informed, in America the portions are so big that usually one portion is equal to enough for two to four individuals. So a few years ago, I decided to lose weight in a big way. Since I know more about diets and nutrition than most people ever even want to know, I decided to get involved in various weight loss programs, boot camp, weight lifting, and gym memberships, and to have accountability partners. What I found is what all of us find that have experience: the programs work. All of them work. I can be successful in any or all of them when I follow the program outlines. It's not about whether or not they work, it's about whether or not one can and will stick with them and whether or not it is the right plan for the individual. No two people are alike, and some things work for some and not others and vice versa.

Something I did in my weight loss was I let people know I was on a weight reduction program to get healthy. Now, I let people know I have lost seventy pounds, what my goals are, and what keeps me focused. I'm not saying that will work for others, but it is working for me. Some individuals have imbalances in hormones or other health issues that keep them from being a healthy weight. For me, lifestyle habits and patterns kept me in poor health. Once I decided to change my mind and health, not necessarily focused on weight but having that as a part of the benefit, I found success. The most significant part was that I made the change out of love for myself and my children, not hatred or disdain for how I looked or how I felt about myself.

Financial power

Financially, the most important change I made was changing my relationship to money. I stay on top of my bills and pay them as they are due without paying unnecessary late charges. If I don't have the money, I don't spend it. Making a transition to using mostly debit cards was one of the most difficult financial transitions for me to date, but I make it work. It's not worth it for me to be in debt and to worry about how I am going to pay my bills. It's important for me to keep negative things at bay so that they do not control my life. Also, it is important for me to give to others. In my giving to others, I create balance in my life and am not as attached to wealth and greed. When I was drowning in financial indebtedness, I did not feel the freedom to give to others in need and felt so stuck in negativity that I didn't see a way out. Once, I found balance, I began to experience blessings. Power comes once we change our own self-limiting beliefs and take action to make things happen.

What I learned

It is up to each person to determine what is right for him/her. When some of my clients have gotten clear on changes they want or need to make, they try them and just test the water, so to speak. If things don't work out quite the way they expected, they take two steps backward and stop the changes for a while. I understand exactly where they are coming from. I received correspondence just a few days ago from a client from long ago that wrote to me saying she is finally leaving her husband. She writes that this time she is ready. I am quick to remind her that whatever she is dealing with is okay. It is up to her if or when to make a change. I have heard it said many, many times that when someone is ready to leave or make a change, he/she will know it. There will be no question. Few are one hundred percent certain of decisions and most have questions that remain. Change is for those who find their power and are willing to take the risk for a better life. For lasting change, one has to be able to be okay with making mistakes.

Chapter Nineteen
Find Laughter in Mistakes

I *Love Lucy* is my favorite television show of all time. Lucille Ball was one of the funniest actresses I have ever watched. In fact, I loved her so much that I named my little dog after her as a very young child. To laugh at her was one of the truly great blessings of my childhood. The true story I am sharing with you next reminds me of her.

A couple of years ago, I had an opportunity to make a lot of money in a short period of time. I accidently overheard some information from someone I trusted about some shirt stays she had purchased at an upscale store where she worked. Well, the story was about some gold shirt/collar stays that had been in the store for years and were discounted, and she had purchased them all and was able to take them to a gold buying store and get $40 each. This resulted in the person getting approximately $1,000 dollars and would be able to get more for all of the collar stays she purchased in this store. Who would have thought, huh?

So I kept this information in the back of my mind, and when I visited Oklahoma City a few weeks later, I found that they had the same upscale store, and I thought they might have some shirt stays.

Well, as luck would have it, I had some extra time to go to the store and found not one, not two or three, but thirty-five boxes of collar stays. They looked like they had been there for a long while, and I asked the saleslady how popular they were, and she said no one ever wanted them. In fact, she could not understand why I would want them.

Before I purchased the collar stays, I called the person I heard about this from, and she gave me a full description of the collar stays. She said they had inscriptions on them. Some had "longevity," others had "luck," others had "stay stiff," and others had "when pigs fly." She said she thought she had purchased all of the gold ones and didn't think any of the stores had any more. She asked me how many they had, and I said several but didn't want to tell her how many; she might want some and purchase them before me. I had to be clever and keep my riches to myself.

Well, since the shirt stays had the very description she gave, I decided to purchase ALL thirty-five of them! As the sales lady rang them up, all I could do was total up the amount of money in my mind I would make from them. Each of the boxes had ten, and ten times forty is four hundred, and four hundred times thirty-five equals fourteen thousand dollars. Yeah, I am so good with that. I only had to spend around $700 to make $14,000. Not bad for a few minutes of work.

After I got back to my hotel room, I pondered, *Surely I can find more shirt stays*. There has to be more of these upscale stores in the U.S. I just have to find them all and before anyone else does, of course. I spent the next two hours surfing the internet to find other stores, and after several calls, I found two stores that had more. I purchased nine from one store in California and five from another store in Las Vegas. The more calls I made, the more excited I became. *I think I must have found my road to success*, I said to myself. The next morning, I got up thinking there must be more, but I had spent all the extra money I had on shirt stays. I thought I could call my son and borrow some money, but he would think I had lost my mind and I can't do that. I could call one of my son's best friends; his dad buys and sells gold for a living, but then my son's friend would be in on it and he might get to the other stores before me and I want all the money myself. He has lots more time than me, and I could miss out on great wealth.

All I could think about was what I could do with an extra $20,000. I could get a new stove, get more wood floors and get rid of the carpet, get a new car, pay off some things, the list went on and on and on.

Then, the next morning I drove by a place that had in huge signs about buying gold. I figured I would sell them in Oklahoma. It would probably be better than trying to fly with thirty-five boxes of these things. That afternoon, after I had finished my work project, I went by and took in several boxes of shirt stays.

Much to my surprise, the gold person tested ones from each box only to discover that they were not real gold. I asked her to try another one, and it was the same thing. I was in disbelief, how could this be? After testing several, she refused to test anymore. It was so unsettling that I finally decided to call my son's friend whose father deals with gold, and he told me to take them all back. Sad about missing out on my mission to get rich, quick, I did just that.

I took the shirt/collar stays back to the upscale store and returned them. Right before going into the store, I got a call from the person who I had initially overheard about the shirt stays only to hear from her that she had tried to get some more money and found that they were not gold. Anyway, I thanked her and told her it was a lesson learned.

I returned the shirt/collar stays and luckily just barely made it to my flight out of Oklahoma City. But it was not over! When I got home the packages kept coming in. I received packages from California and Nevada and calls from each of the stores asking if I wanted more. Each time, I received a package or call, I would think about my trip and thoroughly decided that the next time I hear something like "When pigs fly," I will say to myself, "Yes, and if it sounds too good to be true, it probably is too good to be true." I will not be so quick to buy into being greedy.

And I will always maintain the gift of the ability to laugh at myself . . . much like the Lucille Ball that I still love so dearly.

What I learned

The freedom to laugh at one's self is truly at the height of self-actualization. To truly be okay with mistakes is one of the greatest gifts I have ever found or been able to share with others. It is a truth of crossing to the other side and feeling the light that is in all of us. It is the freedom just to be.

Chapter Twenty
See Clearly

"The eyes are the window to the soul." I am not sure when I first heard that statement, but in my experiences, I have found it to be true. Being a mother and close to my children, I can tell when they are happy, sick, tired, or just not doing well by looking into their eyes. My mother did the same; she could tell just by looking into my eyes whether I was sick, happy, or even being dishonest with her. In fact, when I was not doing well, I would keep my distance from her so that she wouldn't worry. I'm not sure, but I wouldn't be surprised if my children did the same thing.

My family of origin tended to be worriers; it had to do with the underlying fear that something bad was going to happen. Of course, with all of the traumatic experiences we had in our childhoods, we were groomed to feel fear around future events. A step beyond this is that when we didn't see clearly, we sometimes created our own crises and dramas. Even though, it may seem not to fit with perfection, it definitely does.

Along with sight, inconsistency has always been a common thread that would enable me to notice issues that sometimes surprised others. It may also be my many years of training and experience as a therapist or my ability to analyze situations well, but if someone is tired, sick, or not doing well and that person tells me he/she is great or fine and their eyes are telling me a different story, it becomes a concern. In my closest relationships with my family and children, I have decided which battles to choose when I am concerned for their well-being. I make it clear, however, that I am available, that I love them, and that I am interested in their lives.

My children are my greatest blessings, bar none. I cannot even imagine my life without them. I am grateful for the miracles that they are and glad that I am clear about how they have enriched my life. Over the years, I have created dramas in their lives, and I'm sure they could have been prevented; I understand it, and the cost to my children was greater than I would have wished. But they have forgiven me, and I have forgiven myself, which is what all parents need to do to move forward.

My oldest son

When my son was a police officer and still lived with me, I had a tendency to worry about him. He was in the Marine Reserves simultaneously with his law enforcement job, and for many years, I had worried about him in that capacity as well. Most of my prayers for him were that God keep him safe. There was this one particular night when he didn't come home. He usually got home around 11:30 or a little later at night, and I was usually asleep when he arrived, but I always woke up when I heard the garage door open, letting me know he was home safely. Well, this particular night I had not awoken to the garage door opening, and when I did wake up, it was close to three the next morning and he was not home. Repeatedly, I called his cell phone and there was no answer. I got into my fear and panicked not knowing what to do so, I reacted. I called the law enforcement number for the county, and the officer there checked and said he left at the usual time. I remember stating that this was not typical for him and that he is usually home by now, but I don't remember saying anything else. Well, that was quite enough! My son had gone to spend the night with a friend, and several police cars filled the front yard and woke them up. He came home not very happy about what I had done and moved out of the house not too long afterwards. Needless to say, I still hear about that episode from time to time, but I don't take it on like I did at that time. Meaning, I don't dislike myself for making that phone call. I am sorry that it involved his job and he had to hear about that episode at work, many times. But he did communicate with me if he was not coming home or coming home late after that night, and he made sure I knew which particular numbers not to call at his job. In fact, he gave me the specific phone number to call in the event that he was missing, which thankfully never happened while he was in law enforcement.

My youngest son

Being a social butterfly, my son has always had an abundance of things to do and friends to be around. He loves new and different things and has friends that he has been close to since elementary school and would always want to go somewhere or do something with them. Well, there was this one time that he didn't come home. At that time, he was probably close to eighteen or even older, and it was before the episode with my oldest son. He was out all night and I did not know where he was; I panicked and took action. Repeatedly, I called his cell phone and there was no answer. I started calling his friends too and finally got in touch with one of his best friend's fathers, who at that time was an army colonel. He informed me, "Our boys are camping." Needless to say, my son was home very soon afterwards—just like the situation with my oldest son. I do not dislike myself now for making that call. I did feel guilty at the time, and I am sorry that it caused him difficulty. Afterwards, he was more informative about where he was going and when he was returning home. To be fair, he told me upon his return that he did tell me of his planned trip, but I do not remember that. However, at that point in time, I was so caught up in my perfection that if I thought I was right, he had to be wrong.

My daughter

A similar situation happened to my daughter when she was right out of high school, if I remember correctly. Our relationship has always been different in that she talks to me often as opposed to once in a while like my sons. Well, there was this one day when she didn't call me back for about four hours, and like with her brothers, I panicked. Repeatedly, I called her friends and kept calling until I got someone on the phone. Finally, I received a call back from her stating that her phone had blown up like a Christmas tree with calls from her friends. She said that her best friend had not only called her and left a message but had called every other friend that she knew and they were all calling her. When I heard my daughter's voice, I felt at peace and that everything was okay. It was the same feeling I had when her brothers had arrived home at times when I did not know they were safe. We laughed about the many calls, then she reassured me that she was fine.

The cost of some decisions

There is no doubt in my mind that working in the field of behavioral health and working at a sexual assault center many years has had its impact on me. There's a great deal of research to support the theory of secondary trauma experienced by those in the helping field. The many true stories about what others have done to hurt innocent people is traumatizing within itself. Hearing the events of real life experience lets us know that it could happen to our families or us.

My three children have seen more death than I have ever seen or been around—one as a police officer, another as a medical doctor, and the other as a nurse. They have dealt with many occurrences stemming from horrific events, accidents, and illnesses. Even though I am so very proud of them for the career paths they have chosen and their willingness to work hard to fulfill their goals, I know it has not come without a cost.

What I have learned

As we are available to our loved ones and others, it's important that we find our own way to be grounded and release the negativity and the pain we've experience. For me, to let go of the perfection and the self-blame for others who experienced pain, I needed to see clearly what my responsibility was and what responsibility belonged to them. Through finding the light, I am now clear. Also, I see clearly that I cannot go back and change anything, but freedom from past suffering and injuries is necessary to move forward. It is also important to know that the barriers and the walls we build between ourselves and those we love take time to collapse and energy to build new structures. For many who take the time and put forth the effort, their relationships can be stronger and healthier. We must remember that in relationships that have been fractured, it will take both sides and a willingness to mend from the past. Thankfully, I have good relationships with each of my children.

In working with many clients, I have found that some of their relationships cannot be mended. When the blame, bitterness, and resentments continue, it's important to go a different path to happiness and acceptance. I have a saying that all of my clients know, and it is very simple: "It's their stuff," meaning it is something for which they (the clients) are not responsible. Some have found new families and new groups of relatives of their choosing; it's a way of being happy and getting their needs met. Once one asks for forgiveness and has done what he/she can do to rectify the situation without causing further pain, the onus is no longer on him/her. I am available to them to help them work through their issues of perfection and negative thinking and whatever other issues they bring to the table.

In my personal life, being surrounded with like-minded positive individuals is easier now that I am a positive person. The individuals that hold on to negativity do not usually stay in my life for very long; either I move away from them or they venture to someone else. The old saying, "misery loves company," comes to mind, and I am much happier not being caught up in negativity, drama, and crises. I have found that those who want to gossip and not communicate openly tend to find others that do the same; for me, choosing not to be a part of that gives me the ability to see clearly as I move on in my purpose and continue *loving myself* in my own imperfection.

Finding the Light

When I found the light, the best way to define it is simply *I found emotional balance*. It was not only that it was simple, it was something that made sense to me. It wasn't that I found what some call enlightenment, but perhaps I did. It wasn't that there was a light bulb moment or that a great thunder rolled or that lightning flashed in the sky, but perhaps it did. Finding the light for me was finding happiness, being content, and having peace. It is being able to live in the real world without fear, to live with the good, the bad, and the ugly, and being content enough not to let the challenges impact me enough to steal my joy. It is about waking up every morning being thankful for another day and thankful for the gifts from God and the universe. It is about bouncing back after conflicts with others and not allowing them to define my next moment or next day. It's about the love I have for my three children, and the joy they bring me just by being the blessings from God that they are. It's about the unwavering love I have for my family and my friends. It's about unconditional love and knowing that I am safe, guided, loved, and protected, that my destiny is not my own and being okay with that. It's about being real and present and open to help others on their paths to find what I have found.

It is important for me to be present for the beauty in life, and when I have taken action where it is needed, I am present and grateful. It is also wonderful to feel God's grace that I never really lost but somehow believed that I had. It was my own self-limiting belief that God wouldn't be there for me, but he never left and was always there.

Today, I walk in peace and joy. I feel the soft wind from the trees as the branches sway to and fro, the warmth of the bright sunshine, and the solid earth beneath my feet. I am firmly grounded. The presence of God and angels are with me like beautiful white light beaming down from the heavens, and I know that I am not alone. Fear does not consume me, and I am thankful. The frightened child I was once exists no more. Sadness, guilt, anger, and shame no longer control me. I have discovered a new day of light within myself and all around. And I am calling forth all who give life, create life, and carry life so that we may bring healing to our planet. It must start with us. Won't you join me?

About the Author

Linda Sue McCall has twenty-eight years of experience with agencies, educational institutions, and private practices where she gained expertise in the fields of mental health, substance abuse, and trauma. She is a former adjunct professor where she taught master's-level counseling students for two years. She has served as an accreditation surveyor at an international company for eight years, surveying behavioral health companies nationally. Linda is a devoted mother and a strong advocate for self-empowerment and wholeness. She believes in alternative and experiential therapies that result in transformational changes; she assists individuals in tapping into their purposes in life, eliminating fears, and developing the power to take action.

Being a change agent, she believes in the power of individuals to make desired life changes. She is a strong role model and mentor to many by living her life of faith and by sharing her challenges as well as her successes. She is not afraid to take risks and walk through the fire if needed for positive growth and to help others. She is a believer that positive change on an individual level impacts society as a whole, by one person at a time. She is a licensed clinical social worker and a 1996 graduate of the University of Georgia. With her first book, she is responding to her calling by sharing her life experiences, what she did about it, and how she has helped others to find the light by releasing perfection.

www.ingramcontent.com/pod-product-compliance
Lightning Source LLC
Chambersburg PA
CBHW062243300426
44110CB00034B/1550